PHILLIS WHEATLEY

FRONTISPIECE FROM THE ORIGINAL EDITION OF THE POEMS

(See p. 100 for more information)

Phillis Wheatley

POEMS ON VARIOUS SUBJECTS,
RELIGIOUS AND MORAL

AND

A MEMOIR OF
PHILLIS WHEATLEY,
A NATIVE AFRICAN
AND A SLAVE

RENARD PRESS

RENARD PRESS LTD

Kemp House
152–160 City Road
London EC1V 2NX
United Kingdom
info@renardpress.com
020 8050 2928

www.renardpress.com

Poems on Various Subjects, Religious and Moral first published in 1773
Memoir of Phillis Wheatley: A Native African and a Slave first published in 1834
This edition first published by Renard Press Ltd in 2020

Edited text © Renard Press Ltd, 2020
Notes, Note on the Text and To the Public © Renard Press Ltd, 2020

Cover design by Will Dady
Proofread by Charlie Morgan

ISBN: 978-1-80447-000-8

The pictures in this volume are reprinted with permission or are presumed to be in the public domain. Every effort has been made to ascertain their copyright status, and to acknowledge this status where required, but we will be happy to correct any errors, should any unwitting oversights have been made, in subsequent editions.

All rights reserved. This publication may not be reproduced, stored in a retrieval system or transmitted, in any form or by any means – electronic, mechanical, photocopying, recording or otherwise – without the prior permission of the publisher. This book is sold subject to the condition that it shall not be resold, lent, hired out or circulated by any other means without the prior written consent of the publisher.

CONTENTS

Phillis Wheatley	7
To the Public	9
Poems on Various Subjects, Religious and Moral	11
To Maecenas	13
On Virtue	15
To the University of Cambridge in New England	16
To the King's Most Excellent Majesty	17
On Being Brought from Africa to America	18
On the Death of the Rev. Dr Sewell	18
On the Death of the Rev. Mr George Whitefield	20
On the Death of a Young Lady of Five Years of Age	22
On the Death of a Young Gentleman	23
To a Lady on the Death of Her Husband	24
Goliath of Gath	26
Thoughts on the Works of Providence	33
To a Lady on the Death of Three Relations	38
To a Clergyman on the Death of His Lady	39
A Hymn to the Morning	41
A Hymn to the Evening	42
Isaiah LXIII 1–8	43
On Recollection	44
On Imagination	46
A Funeral Poem on the Death of C.E.	48
To Captain H——D of the 65th Regiment	50

To the Right Honourable William, Earl of Dartmouth	50
Ode to Neptune	52
To a Lady on Her Coming to North America	53
To a Lady on Her Remarkable Preservation in a Hurricane in North Carolina	55
To a Lady and Her Children on the Death of Her Son and Their Brother	56
To a Gentleman and Lady on the Death of the Lady's Brother and Sister, and a Child	57
On the Death of Dr Samuel Marshall	59
To a Gentleman on His Voyage to Great Britain	60
To the Rev. Dr Thomas Amory	61
On the Death of J.C., an Infant	63
A Hymn to Humanity	64
To the Honourable T.H., Esq., on the Death of His Daughter	66
Niobe in Distress for Her Children Slain by Apollo	68
To S.M., a Young African Painter	75
To His Honour the Lieutenant Governor, on the Death of His Lady	77
A Farewell to America	79
A Rebus, by I.B.	82
An Answer to the Rebus	83
A Memoir of Phillis Wheatley, a Native African and a Slave	85
Note on the Text	109
Notes	110
Index of First Lines	117
Appendix	119
Preface from the First Edition of the Poems	121
Notice to the Public from the First Edition of the Poems	123
Notice to the Public from the First Edition of the Memoir	125

PHILLIS WHEATLEY

Poems on Various Subjects,
Religious and Moral

and

A Memoir of Phillis Wheatley,
a Native African and a Slave

TO THE PUBLIC

In 1761, a slave ship called *The Phillis* docked at Boston harbour, having made a slow and tortuous journey from West Africa to the British colony of Massachusetts. On this boat was a seven-year-old girl, who was sold to the well-to-do Wheatley family in Boston; the family's slaves were growing old, and they wanted a young domestic slave to keep them company in their dotage. Thus Phillis Wheatley was born – renamed after the ship which tore her from her family and the family whose property she became.

Phillis was adored by the family – Susanna Wheatley, in particular – and they helped her to learn English and allowed her to study the classics. Just like Terence, the Roman playwright she writes of, Phillis was brought as a slave to a strange city far from home, and showed such a natural aptitude for language that her owners granted her her freedom.

As related in the 1834 memoir republished in this volume, by Benjamin Bussey Thatcher (1809–40), an outspoken proponent of antislavery, the road to publication was not straight, and early biographers point out that much of Phillis' poetry may be unknown, since she had such an appetite for writing that she would even do so with chalk on the Wheatleys' walls, not having the paper to commit her words to. Once her talent became known and the Wheatleys began to encourage her writing, she was met with real disbelief.

In 1772, she was interrogated by a panel and forced to defend the ownership of her own words, since many believed that it was an impossible that she, an African-American slave, could write poetry of such high quality. This view was so prevalent, so acceptable, that the first publisher prefaced the volume of poetry with an 'attestation from the most respectable characters in Boston, that none might have the least ground for disputing' their authorship.

In publishing this volume in 2020, moving the attestation of authorship to the end of the book, along with the 'letter from her master' and condescending note from the original publishers of the memoir and the poems, it is this Publisher's fervent hope that the twenty-first-century reader can discover Phillis Wheatley as she should always have been read – as a poet, not property.

– RENARD PRESS, 2020

POEMS ON VARIOUS SUBJECTS, RELIGIOUS AND MORAL

TO THE RIGHT HONOURABLE THE
COUNTESS OF HUNTINGDON,
THE FOLLOWING
POEMS
ARE MOST RESPECTFULLY INSCRIBED
BY HER MUCH OBLIGED,
VERY HUMBLE
AND DEVOTED SERVANT,
PHILLIS WHEATLEY

TO MAECENAS*

Maecenas, you, beneath the myrtle shade,
Read o'er what poets sung and shepherds play'd.
What felt those poets but you feel the same?
Does not your soul possess the sacred flame?
Their noble strains your equal genius shares
In softer language and diviner airs.

   While Homer paints, lo! circumfus'd in air,
Celestial Gods in mortal forms appear;
Swift as they move hear each recess rebound,
Heav'n quakes, earth trembles and the shores resound.   10
Great sire of verse, before my mortal eyes,
The lightnings blaze across the vaulted skies,
And, as the thunder shakes the heav'nly plains,
A deep-felt horror thrills through all my veins.
When gentler strains demand thy graceful song,
The length'ning line moves languishing along.
When great Patroclus courts Achilles' aid,*
The grateful tribute of my tears is paid;
Prone on the shore he feels the pangs of love,
And stern Pelides'* tend'rest passions move.   20

   Great Maro's strain in heav'nly numbers flows,
The nine* inspire, and all the bosom glows.*
O could I rival thine and Virgil's page,
Or claim the muses with the Mantuan sage;*
Soon the same beauties should my mind adorn,
And the same ardours in my soul should burn:
Then should my song in bolder notes arise,

And all my numbers pleasingly surprise;
But here I sit, and mourn a grov'lling mind,
That fain would mount, and ride upon the wind.   30

    Not you, my friend, these plaintive strains become,
Not you, whose bosom is the muses' home;
When they from tow'ring Helicon* retire,
They fan in you the bright immortal fire,
But I, less happy, cannot raise the song –
The fault'ring music dies upon my tongue.

    The happier Terence[1] all the choir inspir'd,*
His soul replenish'd and his bosom fir'd;
But say, ye muses, why this partial grace,
To one alone of Afric's sable race;   40
From age to age transmitting thus his name
With the finest glory in the rolls of fame?

    Thy virtues, great Maecenas, shall be sung
In praise of him, from whom those virtues sprung;
While blooming wreaths around thy temples spread,
I'll snatch a laurel from thine honour'd head,
While you indulgent smile upon the deed.

    As long as Thames in streams majestic flows,
Or naiads in their oozy beds repose,*
While Phoebus* reigns above the starry train,   50
While bright Aurora* purples o'er the main,
So long, great sir, the muse thy praise shall sing,
So long thy praise shall make Parnassus* ring –
Then grant, Maecenas, thy paternal rays;
Hear me propitious, and defend my lays.

---

1 He was an African by birth.

ON VIRTUE

O thou bright jewel, in my aim I strive
To comprehend thee. Thine own words declare
Wisdom is higher than a fool can reach.
I cease to wonder, and no more attempt
Thine height t'explore, or fathom thy profound.
But, O my soul, sink not into despair;
Virtue is near thee, and with gentle hand
Would now embrace thee – hovers o'er thine head.
Fain would the heav'n-born soul with her converse,
Then seek, then court her for her promis'd bliss.

Auspicious queen, thine heav'nly pinions spread,
And lead celestial Chastity along;
Lo! now her sacred retinue descends,
Array'd in glory from the orbs above.
Attend me, Virtue, thro' my youthful years!
O leave me not to the false joys of time,
But guide my steps to endless life and bliss.
Greatness, or Goodness, say what I shall call thee,
To give me a higher appellation still,
Teach me a better strain, a nobler lay,
O thou, enthron'd with cherubs in the realms of day.

TO THE UNIVERSITY OF
CAMBRIDGE IN NEW ENGLAND*

While an intrinsic ardour prompts to write,
The muses promise to assist my pen;
'Twas not long since I left my native shore –
The land of errors and Egyptian gloom;
Father of mercy, 'twas thy gracious hand
Brought me in safety from those dark abodes.

Students, to you 'tis giv'n to scan the heights
Above, to traverse the ethereal space,
And mark the systems of revolving worlds.
Still more, ye sons of science, ye receive   10
The blissful news by messengers from heav'n,
How Jesus' blood for your redemption flows.
See him with hands outstretcht upon the cross;
Immense compassion in his bosom glows;
He hears revilers, nor resents their scorn:
What matchless mercy in the Son of God!
When the whole human race by sin had fall'n,
He deign'd to die that they might rise again
And share with him, in the sublimest skies,
Life without death, and glory without end.   20

Improve your privileges while they stay,
Ye pupils, and each hour redeem, that bears
Or good or bad report of you to heav'n.

Let sin, that baneful evil to the soul,
By you be shunn'd, nor once remit your guard;
Suppress the deadly serpent in its egg.
Ye blooming plants of human race divine,
An Ethiop* tells you 'tis your greatest foe;
Its transient sweetness turns to endless pain,
And in immense perdition sinks the soul.   30

TO THE KING'S MOST EXCELLENT MAJESTY

Your subjects hope, dread sire,
The crown upon your brows may flourish long,
And that your arm may in your God be strong!
O may your sceptre num'rous nations sway,
And all with love and readiness obey!

But how shall we the British King reward?
Rule thou in peace, our father and our lord!
Midst the remembrance of thy favours past,
The meanest peasants most admire the last.[1]*
May George, beloved by all the nations round,
Live with Heav'n's choicest constant blessings crown'd!
Great God, direct and guard him from on high,
And from his head let ev'ry evil fly!
And may each clime with equal gladness see
A monarch's smile can set his subjects free!

1768

---

[1] The Repeal of the Stamp Act.

ON BEING BROUGHT FROM AFRICA TO AMERICA

'Twas mercy brought me from my pagan land,
Taught my benighted soul to understand
That there's a God – that there's a Saviour too;
Once I redemption neither fought nor knew;
Some view our sable race with scornful eye:
'Their colour is a diabolic dye!'
Remember, Christians: Negroes, black as Cain,*
May be refin'd, and join th'angelic train.

ON THE DEATH OF THE REV. DR SEWELL

Ere yet the morn its lovely blushes spread,
See Sewell number'd with the happy dead.
Hail, holy man, arriv'd th'immortal shore,
Though we shall hear thy warning voice no more.
Come, let us all behold with wishful eyes
The saint ascending to his native skies;
From hence the prophet wing'd his rapt'rous way
To the blest mansions in eternal day.
Then, begging for the Spirit of our God,
And panting eager for the same abode,   10

ON THE DEATH OF THE REV. DR SEWELL

Come, let us all with the same vigour rise,
And take a prospect of the blissful skies;
While on our minds Christ's image is imprest,
And the dear Saviour glows in ev'ry breast.
Thrice happy saint! to find thy heav'n at last –
What compensation for the evils past!

Great God, incomprehensible, unknown,
By sense, we bow at thine exalted throne.
O, while we beg thine excellence to feel,
Thy sacred Spirit to our hearts reveal, 20
And give us of that mercy to partake,
Which thou hast promis'd for the Saviour's sake!

'Sewell is dead!' swift-pinion'd Fame thus cry'd.
'Is Sewell dead?' my trembling tongue reply'd.
O, what a blessing in his flight deny'd!
How oft for us the holy prophet pray'd!
How oft to us the word of Life convey'd!
By duty urg'd my mournful verse to close,
I for his tomb this epitaph compose:

'Lo, here a man, redeem'd by Jesus' blood, 30
A sinner once, but now a saint with God;
Behold ye rich, ye poor, ye fools, ye wise,
Not let his monument your heart surprise;
'Twill tell you what this holy man has done,
Which gives him brighter lustre than the sun.
Listen, ye happy, from your seats above!
I speak sincerely, while I speak and love;
He fought the paths of piety and truth,

By these made happy from his early youth;
In blooming years that grace divine he felt, 40
Which rescues sinners from the chains of guilt.
Mourn him, ye indigent, whom he has fed,
And henceforth seek, like him, for living bread;
Ev'n Christ, the bread descending from above,
And ask an int'rest in his saving love.
Mourn him, ye youth, to whom he oft has told
God's gracious wonders from the times of old.
I too have cause this mighty loss to mourn,
For he my monitor will not return.
O, when shall we to his blest state arrive? 50
When the same graces in our bosoms thrive.'

1769

ON THE DEATH OF THE REV. MR GEORGE WHITEFIELD

Hail, happy saint, on thine immortal throne,
Possest of glory, life and bliss unknown;
We hear no more the music of thy tongue;
Thy wonted auditories cease to throng.
Thy sermons in unequall'd accents flow'd,
And ev'ry bosom with devotion glow'd;
Thou didst in strains of eloquence refin'd
Inflame the heart and captivate the mind.
Unhappy we the setting sun deplore –
So glorious once, but ah! it shines no more. 10

ON THE DEATH OF THE REV. MR GEORGE WHITEFIELD

Behold the prophet in his tow'ring flight!
He leaves the earth for heav'n's unmeasur'd height,
And worlds unknown receive him from our sight.
There Whitefield wings with rapid course his way,
And sails to Zion* through vast seas of day.
Thy pray'rs, great saint, and thine incessant cries
Have pierc'd the bosom of thy native skies.
Thou moon hast seen, and all the stars of light,
How he has wrestled with his god by night.
He pray'd that grace in ev'ry heart might dwell;   20
He long'd to see America excel;
He charg'd its youth that ev'ry grace divine
Should with full lustre in their conduct shine;
That Saviour, which his soul did first receive
The greatest gift that ev'n a god can give,
He freely offer'd to the num'rous throng
That on his lips with list'ning pleasure hung.

'Take him, ye wretched, for your only good;
Take him ye starving sinners, for your food;
Ye thirsty, come to this life-giving stream;   30
Ye preachers, take him for your joyful theme;
Take him, my dear Americans, he said;
Be your complaints on his kind bosom laid;
Take him, ye Africans, he longs for you;
Impartial Saviour is his title due;
Wash'd in the fountain of redeeming blood,
You shall be sons and kings and priests to God.'

Great Countess,[1] we Americans revere
Thy name, and mingle in thy grief sincere;
New England deeply feels, the orphans mourn,   40
Their more-than-father will no more return.

---
[1] The Countess of Huntingdon, to whom Mr Whitefield was Chaplain.

But, though arrested by the hand of death,
Whitefield no more exerts his lab'ring breath,
Yet let us view him in th'eternal skies;
Let ev'ry heart to this bright vision rise;
While the tomb safe retains its sacred trust,
Till life divine reanimates his dust.

1770

ON THE DEATH OF A YOUNG LADY OF FIVE YEARS OF AGE

From dark abodes to fair ethereal light
Th'enraptur'd innocent has wing'd her flight;
On the kind bosom of eternal love
She finds unknown beatitude above.
This known, ye parents, nor her loss deplore:
She feels the iron hand of pain no more;
The dispensations of unerring grace
Should turn your sorrows into grateful praise;
Let then no tears for her henceforward flow,
No more distress'd in our dark vale below. 10

Her morning sun, which rose divinely bright,
Was quickly mantled with the gloom of night;
But hear in heav'n's blest bow'rs your Nancy fair,
And learn to imitate her language there.
'Thou, Lord, whom I behold with glory crown'd,
By what sweet name, and in what tuneful sound
Wilt thou be prais'd? Seraphic pow'rs are faint

Infinite love and majesty to paint.
To thee let all their graceful voices raise,
And saints and angels join their songs of praise.'   20

Perfect in bliss she from her heav'nly home
Looks down, and smiling beckons you to come;
Why then, fond parents – why these fruitless groans?
Restrain your tears and cease your plaintive moans.
Freed from a world of sin and snares and pain –
Why would you wish your daughter back again?
No – bow resign'd. Let hope your grief control,
And check the rising tumult of the soul.
Calm in the prosperous and adverse day;
Adore the God who gives and takes away;   30
Eye Him in all, His holy name revere,
Upright your actions, and your hearts sincere,
Till having sail'd through life's tempestuous sea,
And from its rocks and boist'rous billows free
Yourselves, safe landed on the blissful shore,
Shall join your happy babe to part no more.

ON THE DEATH OF A YOUNG GENTLEMAN

Who taught thee conflict with the pow'rs of night,
To vanquish Satan in the fields of light?
Who strung thy feeble arms with might unknown?
How great thy conquest, and how bright thy crown!
War with each princedom, throne and pow'r is o'er,

The scene is ended to return no more.
O could my muse thy seat on high behold,
How deckt with laurel, how enrich'd with gold!
O could she hear what praise thine harp employs —
How sweet thine anthems, how divine thy joys! 10
What heav'nly grandeur should exalt her strain!
What holy raptures in her numbers reign!
To soothe the troubles of the mind to peace,
To still the tumult of life's tossing seas,
To ease the anguish of the parent's heart,
What shall my sympathising verse impart?
Where is the balm to heal so deep a wound?
Where shall a sov'reign remedy be found?
Look, gracious spirit, from thine heav'nly bow'r,
And thy full joys into their bosoms pour; 20
The raging tempest of their grief control,
And spread the dawn of glory through the soul,
To eye the path the saint departed trod
And trace him to the bosom of his god.

TO A LADY ON THE DEATH OF HER HUSBAND

Grim monarch! see, depriv'd of vital breath,
A young physician in the dust of death:
Dost thou go on incessant to destroy,
Our griefs to double and lay waste our joy?
Enough thou never yet wast known to say,

TO A LADY ON THE DEATH OF HER HUSBAND

Though millions die – the vassals of thy sway;
Nor youth, nor science, nor the ties of love,
Nor ought on earth thy flinty heart can move.
The friend, the spouse from his dire dart to save,
In vain we ask the sovereign of the grave.   10
Fair mourner, there see thy lov'd Leonard laid,
And o'er him spread the deep impervious shade.
Clos'd are his eyes, and heavy fetters keep
His senses bound in never-waking sleep,
Till time shall cease, till many a starry world
Shall fall from heav'n, in dire confusion hurl'd,
Till nature in her final wreck shall lie,
And her last groan shall rend the azure sky.
Not, not till then his active soul shall claim
His body, a divine immortal frame.   20

But see the softly stealing tears apace
Pursue each other down the mourner's face;
But cease thy tears, bid ev'ry sigh depart
And cast the load of anguish from thine heart:
From the cold shell of his great soul arise,
And look beyond, thou native of the skies –
There fix thy view, where fleeter than the wind
Thy Leonard mounts, and leaves the earth behind.
Thyself prepare to pass the vale of night
To join for ever on the hills of light: 30
To thine embrace this joyful spirit moves
To thee, the partner of his earthly loves;
He welcomes thee to pleasures more refin'd
And better suited to th'immortal mind.

GOLIATH OF GATH*

1 Samuel VII

Ye martial pow'rs, and all ye tuneful nine,
Inspire my song and aid my high design.
The dreadful scenes and toils of war I write,
The ardent warriors and the fields of fight:
You best remember, and you best can sing
The acts of heroes to the vocal string;
Resume the lays with which your sacred lyre
Did then the poet and the sage inspire.

   Now front to front the armies were display'd,
Here Israel rang'd, and there the foes array'd;   10
The hosts on two opposing mountains stood,
Thick as the foliage of the waving wood;
Between them an extensive valley lay,
O'er which the gleaming armour pour'd the day,
When from the camp of the Philistine foes,
Dreadful to view, a mighty warrior rose;
In the dire deeds of bleeding battle skill'd,
The monster stalks the terror of the field.
From Gath he sprung – Goliath was his name:
Of fierce deportment and gigantic frame;   20
A brazen helmet on his head was plac'd;
A coat of mail his form terrific grac'd;
The greaves his legs, the targe his shoulders prest:*
Dreadful in arms high-tow'ring o'er the rest
A spear he proudly wav'd, whose iron head,

26

Strange to relate, six hundred shekels weigh'd;
He strode along, and shook the ample field,
While Phoebus blaz'd refulgent on his shield:
Through Jacob's race* a chilling horror ran,
When thus the huge, enormous chief began: 30

   'Say, what the cause that in this proud array
You set your battle in the face of day?
One hero find in all your vaunting train,
Then see who loses, and who wins the plain;
For he who wins in triumph may demand
Perpetual service from the vanquish'd land;
Your armies I defy, your force despise,
By far inferior in Philistia's* eyes!
Produce a man, and let us try the fight,
Decide the contest and the victor's right.' 40

   Thus challeng'd he; all Israel stood amaz'd,
And ev'ry chief in consternation gaz'd;
But Jesse's son* in youthful bloom appears,
And warlike courage far beyond his years:
He left the folds, he left the flow'ry meads,
And soft recesses of the sylvan shades.
Now Israel's monarch and his troops arise,
With peals of shouts ascending to the skies;
In Elah's vale the scene of combat lies.

   When the fair morning blush'd with orient red, 50
What David's fire enjoin'd the son obey'd,
And swift of foot towards the trench he came,
Where glow'd each bosom with the martial flame.
He leaves his carriage to another's care
And runs to greet his brethren of the war.
While yet they spake the giant-chief arose,

Repeats the challenge and insults his foes;
Struck with the sound and trembling at the view,
Affrighted Israel from its post withdrew.
'Observe ye this tremendous foe,' they cry'd, 60
'Who in proud vaunts our armies hath defy'd:
Whoever lays him prostrate on the plain,
Freedom in Israel for his house shall gain;
And on him wealth unknown the King will pour,
And give his royal daughter for his dow'r.'

Then Jesse's youngest hope: 'My brethren, say,
What shall be done for him who takes away
Reproach from Jacob — who destroys the chief
And puts a period to his country's grief?
He vaunts the honours of his arms abroad 70
And scorns the armies of the living God!'

Thus spoke the youth; th'attentive people ey'd
The wond'rous hero, and again reply'd:
'Such the rewards our monarch will bestow
On him who conquers and destroys his foe.'

Eliab* heard, and kindled into ire
To hear his shepherd brother thus inquire,
And thus begun: 'What errand brought thee? Say,
Who keeps thy flock? Or does it go astray?
I know the base ambition of thine heart, 80
But back in safety from the field depart.'

Eliab thus to Jesse's youngest heir
Express'd his wrath in accents most severe.
When to his brother mildly he reply'd:
'What have I done? Or what the cause to chide?'

The words were told before the King, who sent
For the young hero to his royal tent;

Before the monarch dauntless he began:
'For this Philistine fail no heart of man:
I'll take the vale, and with the giant fight;   90
I dread not all his boasts, nor all his might.'
When thus the King: 'Dar'st thou a stripling go,
And venture combat with so great a foe,
Who all his days has been inur'd to fight,
And made its deeds his study and delight?
Battles and bloodshed brought the monster forth,
And clouds and whirlwinds usher'd in his birth.'
When David thus: 'I kept the fleecy care,
And out there rush'd a lion and a bear;
A tender lamb the hungry lion took,   100
And with no other weapon than my crook
Bold I pursu'd, and chas'd him o'er the field –
The prey deliver'd, and the felon kill'd;
As thus the lion and the bear I slew,
So shall Goliath fall, and all his crew!
The God, who sav'd me from these beasts of prey,
By me this monster in the dust shall lay.'
So David spoke. The wond'ring King reply'd:
'Go thou with Heav'n and victory on thy side –
This coat of mail, this sword gird on,' he said,   110
And plac'd a mighty helmet on his head.
The coat, the sword, the helm he laid aside,
Nor chose to venture with those arms untry'd;
Then took his staff, and to the neighb'ring brook
Instant he ran, and thence five pebbles took.
Meantime descended to Philistia's son
A radiant cherub, and he thus begun:
'Goliath, well thou know'st thou hast defy'd

Yon Hebrew armies, and their God deny'd –
Rebellious wretch! audacious worm! forbear,   120
Nor tempt the vengeance of their God too far;
Them, who with His Omnipotence contend,
No eye shall pity, and no arm defend.
Proud as thou art, in short-liv'd glory great,
I come to tell thee thine approaching fate.
Regard my words. The Judge of all the gods,
Beneath whose steps the tow'ring mountain nods,
Will give thine armies to the savage brood
That cut the liquid air or range the wood.
Thee too a well-aim'd pebble shall destroy,   130
And thou shalt perish by a beardless boy.
Such is the mandate from the realms above,
And should I try the vengeance to remove,
Myself a rebel to my king would prove.
Goliath, say, shall grace to him be shown,
Who dares heav'ns Monarch, and insults his throne?'

   'Your words are lost on me,' the giant cries,
While fear and wrath contended in his eyes.
When thus the messenger from heav'n replies:
'Provoke no more Jehovah's awful hand   140
To hurl its vengeance on thy guilty land:
He grasps the thunder, and he wings the storm,
Servants their sov'reign's orders to perform.'

   The angel spoke, and turn'd his eyes away,
Adding new radiance to the rising day.

   Now David comes: the fatal stones demand
His left; the staff engag'd his better hand;
The giant mov'd, and from his tow'ring height
Survey'd the stripling and disdain'd the fight –

And thus began: 'Am I a dog with thee? 150
Bring'st thou no armour, but a staff to me?
The gods on thee their volleyed curses pour,
And beasts and birds of prey thy flesh devour.'

   David undaunted thus: 'Thy spear and shield
Shall no protection to thy body yield:
Jehovah's name – no other arms I bear;
I ask no other in this glorious war.
Today the Lord of Hosts to me will give
Vict'ry; today thy doom thou shalt receive;
The fate you threaten shall your own become, 160
And beasts shall be your animated tomb –
That all the earth's inhabitants may know
That there's a god who governs all below;
This great assembly too shall witness stand,
That needs nor sword, nor spear, th'Almighty's hand:
The battle his, the conquest he bestows,
And to our pow'r consigns our hated foes.'

   Thus David spoke; Goliath heard and came
To meet the hero in the field of fame.
Ah! fatal meeting to thy troops and thee, 170
But thou wast deaf to the divine decree;
Young David meets thee, meets thee not in vain;
'Tis thine to perish on th'ensanguin'd plain.

   And now the youth the forceful pebble slung;
Philistia trembled as it whizz'd along;
In his dread forehead, where the helmet ends,
Just o'er the brows the well-aim'd stone descends –
It pierc'd the skull and shatter'd all the brain;
Prone on his face he tumbled to the plain:
Goliath's fall no smaller terror yields 180

Than riving thunders in aerial fields;
The soul still ling'red in its lov'd abode,
Till conq'ring David o'er the giant strode;
Goliath's sword then laid its master dead,
And from the body hew'd the ghastly head;
The blood in gushing torrents drench'd the plains;
The soul found passage through the spouting veins.

  And now aloud th'illustrious victor said,
'Where are your boastings now your champion's dead?'
Scarce had he spoke when the Philistines fled –   190
But fled in vain: the conqu'ror swift pursu'd;
What scenes of slaughter! and what seas of blood!
There Saul* thy thousands grasp'd th'impurpled sand
In pangs of death the conquest of thine hand;
And David there were thy ten thousands laid –
Thus Israel's damsels musically play'd.

  Near Gath and Edron many a hero lay,
Breath'd out their souls and curs'd the light of day:
Their fury, quench'd by death, no longer burns,
And David with Goliath's head returns,   200
To Salem* brought, but in his tent he plac'd
The load of armour which the giant grac'd.
His monarch saw him coming from the war,
And thus demanded of the son of Ner:*
'Say, who is this amazing youth?' he cry'd,
When thus the leader of the host reply'd:
'As lives thy soul I know not whence he sprung,
So great in prowess, though in years so young.'
'Enquire whose son is he,' the sov'reign said,
'Before whose conq'ring arm Philistia fled.'   210
Before the King behold the stripling stand,

Goliath's head depending from his hand;
To him the King: 'Say of what martial line
Art thou, young hero, and what sire was thine?'
He humbly thus: 'The son of Jesse, I:
I came the glories of the field to try.
Small is my tribe, but valiant in the fight;
Small is my city, but thy royal right.'
'Then take the promis'd gifts,' the monarch cry'd,
Conferring riches and the royal bride; 220
'Knit to my soul – for ever thou remain
With me, nor quit my regal roof again.'

THOUGHTS ON THE WORKS OF PROVIDENCE

Arise, my soul, on wings enraptur'd rise
To praise the Monarch of the earth and skies –
Whose goodness and beneficence appear
As round its centre moves the rolling year,
Or when the morning glows with rosy charms,
Or the sun slumbers in the ocean's arms;
Of light divine be a rich portion lent
To guide my soul, and favour my intent.
Celestial muse, my arduous flight sustain
And raise my mind to a seraphic strain! 10
   Ador'd for ever be the God unseen,
Which round the sun revolves this vast machine,
Though to His eye its mass a point appears;

Ador'd the God that whirls surrounding spheres,
Which first ordain'd that mighty Sol* should reign –
The peerless monarch of th'ethereal train:
Of miles twice forty millions is his height,
And yet his radiance dazzles mortal sight
So far beneath – from him th'extended earth
Vigour derives, and ev'ry flow'ry birth: 20
Vast through her orb she moves with easy grace
Around her Phoebus in unbounded space;
True to her course th'impetuous storm derides,
Triumphant o'er the winds and surging tides.

   Almighty, in these wond'rous works of thine,
What pow'r, what wisdom and what goodness shine!
And are thy wonders, Lord, by men explor'd,
And yet creating glory unador'd!

   Creation smiles in various beauty gay,
While day to night, and night succeeds to day: 30
That wisdom, which attends Jehovah's ways,
Shines most conspicuous in the solar rays;
Without them, destitute of heat and light,
This world would be the reign of endless night –
In their excess how would our race complain,
Abhorring life! how hate its length'ned chain!
From air adust what num'rous ills would rise?
What dire contagion taint the burning skies?
What pestilential vapours, fraught with death,
Would rise, and overspread the lands beneath? 40

   Hail, smiling morn, that from the orient main
Ascending dost adorn the heav'nly plain!
So rich, so various are thy beauteous dies,

That spread through all the circuit of the skies,
That, full of thee, my soul in rapture soars,
And thy great god, the cause of all adores.

   O'er beings infinite his love extends,
His wisdom rules them and his pow'r defends.
When tasks diurnal tire the human frame,
The spirits faint, and dim the vital flame – 50
Then, too, that ever-active bounty shines,
Which not infinity of space confines.
The sable veil, that night in silence draws,
Conceals effects, but shows th'Almighty Cause;
Night seals in sleep the wide creation fair,
And all is peaceful but the brow of care.
Again, gay Phoebus, as the day before,
Wakes ev'ry eye but what shall wake no more;
Again the face of nature is renew'd,
Which still appears harmonious, fair and good. 60
May grateful strains salute the smiling morn,
Before its beams the eastern hills adorn!

   Shall day to day, and night to night conspire
To show the goodness of the Almighty Sire?
This mental voice shall man regardless hear,
And never, never raise the filial pray'r?
Today, O hearken, nor your folly mourn
For time misspent, that never will return.

   But see the sons of vegetation rise
And spread their leafy banners to the skies. 70
All-wise Almighty Providence we trace
In trees and plants, and all the flow'ry race;
As clear as in the nobler frame of man,

All lovely copies of the Maker's plan.
The pow'r the same that forms a ray of light,
That call'd creation from eternal night.
'Let there be light,' he said: from his profound
Old Chaos heard, and trembled at the sound;
Swift as the word, inspir'd by pow'r divine,
Behold the light around its Maker shine –   80
The first fair product of th'omnific God,
And now through all his works diffus'd abroad.

  As reason's pow'rs by day our God disclose,
So we may trace Him in the night's repose:
Say, what is sleep? And dreams how passing strange!
When action ceases, and ideas range
Licentious and unbounded o'er the plains,
Where Fancy's queen in giddy triumph reigns.
Hear in soft strains the dreaming lover sigh
To a kind fair, or rave in jealousy;   90
On pleasure now, and now on vengeance bent,
The lab'ring passions struggle for a vent.
What pow'r, O man, thy reason then restores!
So long suspended in nocturnal hours?
What secret hand returns the mental train,
And gives improv'd thine active pow'rs again?
From thee, O man, what gratitude should rise!
And, when from balmy sleep thou op'st thine eyes,
Let thy first thoughts be praises to the skies.
How merciful our God who thus imparts   100
O'erflowing tides of joy to human hearts,
When wants and woes might be our righteous lot,
Our God forgetting, by our God forgot!

Among the mental pow'rs a question rose –
'What most the image of th'Eternal shows?'
When thus to Reason (so let Fancy rove)
Her great companion spoke, immortal Love:
  'Say, mighty pow'r, how long shall strife prevail,
And with its murmurs load the whisp'ring gale?
Refer the cause to Recollection's shrine,   110
Who loud proclaims my origin divine,
The cause whence heav'n and earth began to be,
And is not man immortalis'd by me?
Reason let this most causeless strife subside.'
Thus Love pronounc'd, and Reason thus reply'd:
  'Thy birth, celestial queen! 'tis mine to own,
In thee resplendent is the Godhead shown;
Thy words persuade, my soul enraptur'd feels
Resistless beauty, which thy smile reveals.'
Ardent she spoke, and, kindling at her charms,   120
She clasp'd the blooming goddess in her arms.
  Infinite Love where'er we turn our eyes
Appears: this ev'ry creature's wants supplies;
This most is heard in Nature's constant voice;
This makes the morn, and this the eve rejoice;
This bids the fost'ring rains and dews descend,
To nourish all, to serve one gen'ral end –
The good of man; yet man ungrateful pays
But little homage, and but little praise.
To him, whose works arry'd with mercy shine,   130
What songs should rise, how constant, how divine!

TO A LADY ON THE DEATH OF THREE RELATIONS

We trace the pow'r of Death from tomb to tomb,
And his are all the ages yet to come.
'Tis his to call the planets from on high,
To blacken Phoebus and dissolve the sky;
His, too, when all in his dark realms are hurl'd
From its firm base to shake the solid world;
His fatal sceptre rules the spacious whole,
And trembling nature rocks from pole to pole.

Awful he moves, and wide his wings are spread –
Behold thy brother number'd with the dead! 10
From bondage freed, the exulting spirit flies
Beyond Olympus and these starry skies.
Lost in our woe for thee, blest shade, we mourn
In vain; to earth thou never must return.
Thy sisters, too, fair mourner, feel the dart
Of Death, and with fresh torture rend thine heart.
Weep not for them, and leave the world behind.

As a young plant by hurricanes up torn,
So near its parent lies the newly born –
But 'midst the bright ethereal train behold: 20
It shines superior on a throne of gold!
Then, mourner, cease; let hope thy tears restrain;
Smile on the tomb, and soothe the raging pain.

On yon blest regions fix thy longing view,
Mindless of sublunary scenes below;
Ascend the sacred mount, in thought arise,
And seek substantial and immortal joys;
Where hope receives, where faith to vision springs,
And raptur'd seraphs tune th'immortal strings
To strains ecstatic. Thou the chorus join, 30
And to thy father tune the praise divine.

TO A CLERGYMAN ON THE DEATH OF HIS LADY

Where contemplation finds her sacred spring,
Where heav'nly music makes the arches ring,
Where virtue reigns unsulli'd and divine,
Where wisdom thron'd, and all the graces shine:
There sits thy spouse amidst the radiant throng,
While praise eternal warbles from her tongue;
There choirs angelic shout her welcome round,
With perfect bliss, and peerless glory crown'd.

While thy dear mate, to flesh no more confin'd,
Exults a blest, a heav'n-ascended mind, 10
Say, in thy breast shall floods of sorrow rise?
Say, shall its torrents overwhelm thine eyes?
Amid the seats of heav'n a place is free,
And angels open their bright ranks for thee –
For thee they wait, and with expectant eye

Thy spouse leans downward from th'empyreal sky:
'O come away,' her longing spirit cries,
'And share with me the raptures of the skies.
Our bliss divine to mortals is unknown;
Immortal life and glory are our own.   20
There too may the dear pledges of our love
Arrive, and taste with us the joys above;
Attune the harp to more than mortal lays,
And join with us the tribute of their praise
To Him, who dy'd stern justice to atone,
And make eternal glory all our own.
He in His death slew ours, and, as He rose,
He crush'd the dire dominion of our foes;
Vain were their hopes to put the God to flight,
Chain us to hell and bar the gates of light.'   30

She spoke, and turn'd from mortal scenes her eyes,
Which beam'd celestial radiance o'er the skies.

Then thou, dear man, no more with grief retire –
Let grief no longer damp devotion's fire,
But rise sublime, to equal bliss aspire,
Thy sighs no more be wafted by the wind,
No more complain, but be to heav'n resign'd.
'Twas thine t'unfold the oracles divine;
To soothe our woes the task was also thine;
Now sorrow is incumbent on thy heart;   40
Permit the muse a cordial to impart;
Who can to thee their tend'rest aid refuse?
To dry thy tears how longs the heav'nly muse!

A HYMN TO THE MORNING

Attend my lays, ye ever honour'd nine;
Assist my labours, and my strains refine;
In smoothest numbers pour the notes along,
For bright Aurora now demands my song.

Aurora hail, and all the thousand dies,
Which deck thy progress through the vaulted skies:
The morn awakes, and wide extends her rays –
On ev'ry leaf the gentle zephyr plays;
Harmonious lays the feather'd race resume;
Dart the bright eye, and shake the painted plume.

Ye shady groves, your verdant gloom display,
To shield your poet from the burning day:
Calliope* awake the sacred lyre,
While thy fair sisters fan the pleasing fire:
The bow'rs, the gales, the variegated skies
In all their pleasures in my bosom rise.

See in the east th'illustrious king of day!
His rising radiance drives the shades away –
But O! I feel his fervid beams too strong,
And scarce begun, concludes th'abortive song.

A HYMN TO THE EVENING

Soon as the sun forsook the eastern main
The pealing thunder shook the heav'nly plain;
Majestic grandeur! from the zephyr's wing,
Exhales the incense of the blooming spring.
Soft purl the streams, the birds renew their notes,
And through the air their mingled music floats.

Through all the heav'ns what beauteous dies are spread!
But the west glories in the deepest red:
So may our breasts with ev'ry virtue glow,
The living temples of our God below!

Fill'd with the praise of Him who gives the light,
And draws the sable curtains of the night,
Let placid slumbers soothe each weary mind,
At morn to wake more heav'nly, more refin'd;
So shall the labours of the day begin,
More pure, more guarded from the snares of sin.

Night's leaden sceptre seals my drowsy eyes,
Then cease, my song, till fair Aurora rise.

ISAIAH LXIII 1–8

Say, heav'nly muse, what king or mighty god,
That moves sublime from Idumea's road?
In Bozrah's* dies, with martial glories join'd,
His purple vesture waves upon the wind.
Why thus enrob'd delights he to appear
In the dread image of the pow'r of war?

Compress'd in wrath the swelling winepress groan'd;
It bled and pour'd the gushing purple round.

'Mine was the act,' th'Almighty Saviour said,
And shook the dazzling glories of His head,   10
'When all forsook I trod the press alone,
And conquer'd by omnipotence my own;
For man's release sustain'd the pond'rous load,
For man the wrath of an immortal God:
To execute th'Eternal's dread command
My soul I sacrific'd with willing hand;
Sinless I stood before the avenging frown,
Atoning thus for vices not my own.'

His eye the ample field of battle round
Survey'd, but no created succours found;   20
His own omnipotence sustain'd the fight;
His vengeance sunk the haughty foes in night;
Beneath his feet the prostrate troops were spread,
And round him lay the dying and the dead.

Great God, what light'ning flashes from thine eyes?
What pow'r withstands if thou indignant rise?

Against thy Zion though her foes may rage,
And all their cunning, all their strength engage,
Yet she serenely on thy bosom lies,
Smiles at their arts, and all their force defies.   30

ON RECOLLECTION

Mneme* begin. Inspire, ye sacred nine,
Your vent'rous Afric in her great design.
Mneme, immortal pow'r, I trace thy spring:
Assist my strains, while I thy glories sing:
The acts of long-departed years, by thee
Recover'd, in due order rang'd we see:
Thy pow'r the long-forgotten calls from night,
That sweetly plays before the fancy's sight.

    Mneme in our nocturnal visions pours
The ample treasure of her secret stores;   10
Swift from above she wings her silent flight
Through Phoebe's realms, fair regent of the night;*
And, in her pomp of images display'd,
To the high-raptur'd poet gives her aid,
Through the unbounded regions of the mind,
Diffusing light celestial and refin'd.
The heav'nly phantom paints the actions done
By ev'ry tribe beneath the rolling sun.

    Mneme, enthron'd within the human breast,
Has vice condemn'd, and ev'ry virtue blest.   20
How sweet the sound when we her plaudit hear?

ON RECOLLECTION

Sweeter than music to the ravish'd ear,
Sweeter than Maro's entertaining strains,
Resounding through the groves and hills and plains.
But how is Mneme dreaded by the race
Who scorn her warnings and despise her grace?
By her unveil'd each horrid crime appears,
Her awful hand a cup of wormwood bears.
Days, years misspent, O what a hell of woe!
Hers the worst tortures that our souls can know. 30

    Now eighteen years their destin'd course have run,
In fast succession round the central sun.
How did the follies of that period pass
Unnotic'd, but behold them writ in brass!
In recollection see them fresh return,
And sure 'tis mine to be asham'd, and mourn.

    O Virtue, smiling in immortal green,
Do thou exert thy pow'r, and change the scene;
Be thine employ to guide my future days,
And mine to pay the tribute of my praise. 40

    Of Recollection such the pow'r enthron'd
In ev'ry breast, and thus her pow'r is own'd.
The wretch, who dar'd the vengeance of the skies,
At last awakes in horror and surprise,
By her alarm'd, he sees impending fate,
He howls in anguish and repents too late.
But O! what peace, what joys are hers t'impart
To ev'ry holy, ev'ry upright heart!
Thrice blest the man who, in her sacred shrine,
Feels himself shelter'd from the wrath divine! 50

ON IMAGINATION

Thy various works, imperial queen, we see –
How bright their forms, how deck'd with pomp by thee!
Thy wond'rous acts in beauteous order stand,
And all attest how potent is thine hand.

From Helicon's refulgent heights attend,
Ye sacred choir, and my attempts befriend:
To tell her glories with a faithful tongue,
Ye blooming graces, triumph in my song.

Now here, now there, the roving Fancy flies,
Till some lov'd object strikes her wand'ring eyes,   10
Whose silken fetters all the senses bind,
And soft captivity involves the mind.

Imagination! who can sing thy force?
Or who describe the swiftness of thy course?
Soaring through air to find the bright abode,
Th'empyreal palace of the thund'ring God,
We on thy pinions can surpass the wind,
And leave the rolling universe behind:
From star to star the mental optics rove,
Measure the skies and range the realms above.   20
There in one view we grasp the mighty whole,
Or with new worlds amaze th'unbounded soul.

ON IMAGINATION

Though winter frowns to Fancy's raptur'd eyes,
The fields may flourish and gay scenes arise;
The frozen deeps may break their iron bands,
And bid their waters murmur o'er the sands.
Fair Flora may resume her fragrant reign,
And with her flow'ry riches deck the plain;
Sylvanus* may diffuse his honours round,
And all the forest may with leaves be crown'd: 30
Show'rs may descend, and dews their gems disclose,
And nectar sparkle on the blooming rose.

Such is thy pow'r, nor are thine orders vain,
O thou the leader of the mental train:
In full perfection all thy works are wrought,
And thine the sceptre o'er the realms of thought.
Before thy throne the subject passions bow,
Of subject passions, sov'reign ruler thou;
At thy command joy rushes on the heart,
And through the glowing veins the spirits dart.   40

Fancy might now her silken pinions try
To rise from earth, and sweep th'expanse on high:
From Tithon's'* bed now might Aurora rise,
Her cheeks all glowing with celestial dyes,
While a pure stream of light o'erflows the skies.
The monarch of the day I might behold,
And all the mountains tipt with radiant gold,
But I reluctant leave the pleasing views,
Which Fancy dresses to delight the muse;
Winter austere forbids me to aspire,   50
And northern tempests damp the rising fire;
They chill the tides of Fancy's flowing sea;
Cease then, my song – cease the unequal lay.

A FUNERAL POEM ON THE DEATH OF C.E.

An Infant of Twelve Months

Through airy roads he wings his instant flight
To purer regions of celestial light;
Enlarg'd he sees unnumber'd systems roll,
Beneath him sees the universal whole;
Planets on planets run their destin'd round,
And circling wonders fill the vast profound.
Th'ethereal now, and now th'empyreal skies
With growing splendours strike his wond'ring eyes:
The angels view him with delight unknown,
Press his soft hand and seat him on his throne;   10
Then, smiling, thus: 'To this divine abode,
The seat of saints, of seraphs and of God,
Thrice welcome thou.' The raptur'd babe replies:
'Thanks to my God, who snatch'd me to the skies,
Ere vice triumphant had possess'd my heart,
Ere yet the tempter had beguil'd my heart,
Ere yet on sin's base actions I was bent,
Ere yet I knew temptation's dire intent;
Ere yet the lash for horrid crimes I felt,
Ere vanity had led my way to guilt,   20
But, soon arriv'd at my celestial goal,
Full glories rush on my expanding soul.'

Joyful he spoke; exulting cherubs round
Clapt their glad wings – the heav'nly vaults resound.

Say, parents, why this unavailing moan?
Why heave your pensive bosoms with the groan?
To Charles, the happy subject of my song,
A brighter world, and nobler strains belong.
Say, would you tear him from the realms above
By thoughtless wishes and prepost'rous love? 30
Doth his felicity increase your pain?
Or could you welcome to this world again
The heir of bliss? With a superior air
Methinks he answers with a smile severe,
'Thrones and dominions cannot tempt me there.'

But still you cry, 'Can we the sigh forbear,
And still and still must we not pour the tear?
Our only hope, more dear than vital breath,
Twelve moons revolv'd, becomes the prey of death;
Delightful infant, nightly visions give 40
Thee to our arms, and we with joy receive;
We fain would clasp the phantom to our breast;
The phantom flies, and leaves the soul unblest.'

To yon bright regions let your faith ascend;
Prepare to join your dearest infant friend
In pleasures without measure, without end.

TO CAPTAIN H———D OF THE 65TH REGIMENT

Say, muse divine, can hostile scenes delight
The warrior's bosom in the fields of fight?
Lo! here the Christian and the hero join
With mutual grace to form the man divine.
In H———D see with pleasure and surprise,
Where valour kindles and where virtue lies:
Go, hero brave, still grace the post of fame,
And add new glories to thine honour'd name;
Still to the field, and still to virtue true:
Britannia glories in no son like you.

TO THE RIGHT HONOURABLE WILLIAM, EARL OF DARTMOUTH*

His Majesty's Principal Secretary of State for North America, etc.

Hail, happy day, when, smiling like the morn,
Fair Freedom rose New England to adorn:
The northern clime beneath her genial ray,
Dartmouth, congratulates thy blissful sway:
Elate with hope her race no longer mourns;
Each soul expands, each grateful bosom burns;
While in thine hand with pleasure we behold

The silken reins, and Freedom's charms unfold.
Long lost to realms beneath the northern skies
She shines supreme, while hated faction dies: 10
Soon as appear'd the goddess long desir'd,
Sick at the view, she languish'd and expir'd;
Thus from the splendours of the morning light
The owl in sadness seeks the caves of night.

No more, America, in mournful strain
Of wrongs, and grievance unredress'd complain,
No longer shalt thou dread the iron chain,
Which wanton Tyranny with lawless hand
Had made, and with it meant t'enslave the land.

Should you, my lord, while you peruse my song, 20
Wonder from whence my love of Freedom sprung –
Whence flow these wishes for the common good,
By feeling hearts alone best understood –
I, young in life, by seeming cruel fate,
Was snatch'd from Afric's fancy'd happy seat:
What pangs excruciating must molest,
What sorrows labour in my parent's breast?
Steel'd was that soul and by no misery mov'd
That from a father seiz'd his babe belov'd:
Such, such my case. And can I then but pray 30
Others may never feel tyrannic sway?

For favours past, great sir, our thanks are due,
And thee we ask thy favours to renew,
Since in thy pow'r, as in thy will before,
To soothe the griefs which thou did'st once deplore.
May heav'nly grace the sacred sanction give
To all thy works, and thou for ever live

Not only on the wings of fleeting Fame,
Though praise immortal crowns the patriot's name,
But to conduct to heav'ns refulgent fane, 40
May fiery coursers sweep th'ethereal plain,
And bear thee upwards to that blest abode,
Where, like the prophet, thou shalt find thy God.

ODE TO NEPTUNE*

On Mrs W.'s Voyage to England

I

While raging tempests shake the shore,
While Aeolus' thunders round us roar*
And sweep impetuous o'er the plain,
Be still, O tyrant of the main;
Nor let thy brow contracted frowns betray
While my Susanna* skims the wat'ry way.

II

The pow'r propitious hears the lay;
The blue-ey'd daughters of the sea
With sweeter cadence glide along;
And Thames responsive joins the song.
Pleas'd with their notes, Sol sheds benign his ray,
And double radiance decks the face of day.

III

To court thee to Britannia's arms,
    Serene the climes and mild the sky,
Her region boasts unnumber'd charms,
    Thy welcome smiles in ev'ry eye.
Thy promise, Neptune, keep, record my pray'r,
Nor give my wishes to the empty air.

              Boston, 12th October, 1772.

TO A LADY ON HER COMING TO NORTH AMERICA

With Her Son for the Recovery of Her Health

Indulgent muse! my grov'lling mind inspire,
And fill my bosom with celestial fire.

See from Jamaica's fervid shore she moves,
Like the fair mother of the blooming loves,
When from above the goddess with her hand
Fans the soft breeze and lights upon the land;
Thus she on Neptune's wat'ry realm reclin'd
Appear'd, and thus invites the ling'ring wind.

'Arise, ye winds, America explore,
Waft me, ye gales, from this malignant shore;   10
The northern milder climes I long to greet,

There hope that health will my arrival meet.'
Soon as she spoke in my ideal view
The winds assented, and the vessel flew.

Madam, your spouse, bereft of wife and son,
In the grove's dark recesses pours his moan;
Each branch, wide-spreading to the ambient sky,
Forgets its verdure, and submits to die.

From thence I turn, and leave the sultry plain,
And swift pursue thy passage o'er the main: 20
The ship arrives before the fav'ring wind,
And makes the Philadelphian port assign'd;
Thence I attend you to Bostonia's arms,
Where gen'rous friendship ev'ry bosom warms:
Thrice welcome here! may health revive again,
Bloom on thy cheek and bound in ev'ry vein!
Then back return to gladden ev'ry heart,
And give your spouse his soul's far dearer part,
Receiv'd again with what a sweet surprise,
The tear in transport starting from his eyes!   30
While his attendant son, with blooming grace,
Springs to his father's ever-dear embrace.
With shouts of joy Jamaica's rocks resound,
With shouts of joy the country rings around.

TO A LADY ON HER REMARKABLE PRESERVATION

In a Hurricane in North Carolina

Though thou did'st hear the tempest from afar,
And felt'st the horrors of the wat'ry war,
To me unknown, yet on this peaceful shore
Methinks I hear the storm tumultuous roar,
And how stern Boreas* with impetuous hand
Compell'd the Nereids* to usurp the land.
Reluctant rose the daughters of the main,
And slow ascending glided o'er the plain,
Till Aeolus in his rapid chariot drove
In gloomy grandeur from the vault above: 10
Furious he comes. His winged sons obey
Their frantic sire, and madden all the sea.
The billows rave, the wind's fierce tyrant roars,
And with his thund'ring terrors shakes the shores:
Broken by waves the vessel's frame is rent,
And strews with planks the wat'ry element.

But thee, Maria, a kind Nereid's shield
Preserv'd from sinking, and thy form upheld:
And sure some heav'nly oracle design'd
At that dread crisis to instruct thy mind 20
Things of eternal consequence to weigh,
And to thine heart just feelings to convey
Of things above, and of the future doom,
And what the births of the dread world to come.

From tossing seas I welcome thee to land.
'Resign her, Nereid,' 'twas thy God's command.
Thy spouse late buried, as thy fears conceiv'd,
Again returns, thy fears are all reliev'd:
Thy daughter blooming with superior grace
Again thou see'st, again thine arms embrace; 30
O come, and joyful show thy spouse his heir,
And what the blessings of maternal care!

TO A LADY AND HER CHILDREN

On the Death of Her Son and Their Brother

O'erwhelming sorrow now demands my song:
From death the overwhelming sorrow sprung.
What flowing tears! what hearts with grief opprest!
What sighs on sighs heave the fond parent's breast!
The brother weeps, the hapless sisters join
Th'increasing woe, and swell the crystal brine;
The poor, who once his gen'rous bounty fed,
Droop, and bewail their benefactor dead.
In death the friend, the kind companion lies,
And in one death what various comfort dies! 10

Th'unhappy mother sees the sanguine rill
Forget to flow, and nature's wheels stand still,
But see from earth his spirit far remov'd,
And know no grief recalls your best belov'd:

He, upon pinions swifter than the wind,
Has left mortality's sad scenes behind
For joys to this terrestrial state unknown,
And glories richer than the monarch's crown.
Of virtue's steady course the prize behold!
What blissful wonders to his mind unfold! 20
But of celestial joys I sing in vain:
Attempt not, muse, the too-advent'rous strain.

No more in briny show'rs ye friends around,
Or bathe his clay, or waste them on the ground:
Still do you weep, still wish for his return?
How cruel thus to wish, and thus to mourn!
No more for him the streams of sorrow pour,
But haste to join him on the heav'nly shore,
On harps of gold to tune immortal lays
And to your God immortal anthems raise. 30

TO A GENTLEMAN AND LADY

On the Death of the Lady's Brother and Sister, and a Child of the Name of Avis, Aged One Year

On Death's domain intent I fix my eyes,
Where human nature in vast ruin lies:
With pensive mind I search the drear abode,
Where the great conqu'ror has his spoils bestow'd;
There where the offspring of six thousand years

In endless numbers to my view appears:
Whole kingdoms in his gloomy den are thrust,
And nations mix with their primeval dust:
Insatiate still he gluts the ample tomb;
His is the present, his the age to come. 10
See here a brother, here a sister spread,
And a sweet daughter mingled with the dead.

But, Madam, let your grief be laid aside,
And let the fountain of your tears be dry'd:
In vain they flow to wet the dusty plain;
Your sighs are wafted to the skies in vain;
Your pains they witness, but they can no more,
While Death reigns tyrant o'er this mortal shore.

The glowing stars and silver queen of light
At last must perish in the gloom of night: 20
Resign thy friends to that Almighty hand,
Which gave them life, and bow to his command;
Thine Avis give without a murm'ring heart,
Though half thy soul be fated to depart.
To shining guards consign thine infant care
To waft triumphant through the seas of air:
Her soul enlarg'd to heav'nly pleasure springs,
She feeds on truth and uncreated things.
Methinks I hear her in the realms above,
And, leaning forward with a filial love, 30
Invite you there to share immortal bliss
Unknown, untasted in a state like this.
With tow'ring hopes, and growing grace arise,
And seek beatitude beyond the skies.

ON THE DEATH OF
DR SAMUEL MARSHALL

Through thickest glooms look back, immortal shade,
On that confusion which thy death has made:
Or from Olympus' height look down, and see
A town involv'd in grief bereft of thee.
Thy Lucy sees thee mingle with the dead,
And rends the graceful tresses from her head,
Wild in her woe, with grief unknown opprest,
Sigh follows sigh deep heaving from her breast.

Too quickly fled, ah! whither art thou gone?
Ah! lost for ever to thy wife and son!   10
The hapless child, thine only hope and heir,
Clings round his mother's neck and weeps his sorrows there.
The loss of thee on Tyler's soul returns,
And Boston for her dear physician mourns.

When sickness call'd for Marshall's healing hand,
With what compassion did his soul expand?
In him we found the father and the friend:
In life how lov'd! how honour'd in his end!

And must not then our Aesculapius* stay
To bring his ling'ring infant into day?   20
The babe unborn in the dark womb is tosst,
And seems in anguish for its father lost.

Gone is Apollo from his house of earth,
But leaves the sweet memorials of his worth:

The common parent, whom we all deplore,
From yonder world unseen must come no more,
Yet 'midst our woes immortal hopes attend
The spouse, the sire, the universal friend.

1771

TO A GENTLEMAN ON HIS VOYAGE

To Great Britain for the Recovery of His Health

While others chant of gay Elysian* scenes,
Of balmy zephyrs and of flow'ry plains,
My song more happy speaks a greater name,
Feels higher motives and a nobler flame.
For thee, O R——, the muse attunes her strings,
And mounts sublime above inferior things.

I sing not now of green embow'ring woods;
I sing not now the daughters of the floods;
I sing not of the storms o'er ocean driv'n,
And how they howl'd along the waste of heav'n.   10
But I to R—— would paint the British shore,
And vast Atlantic, not untry'd before;
Thy life impair'd commands thee to arise,
Leave these bleak regions and inclement skies,
Where chilling winds return the winter past,
And nature shudders at the furious blast.

O thou stupendous, earth-enclosing main,
Exert thy wonders to the world again!
If ere thy pow'r prolong'd the fleeting breath,
Turn'd back the shafts and mock'd the gates of death, 20
If ere thine air dispens'd a healing pow'r,
Or snatch'd the victim from the fatal hour,
This equal case demands thine equal care,
And equal wonders may this patient share.
But unavailing, frantic is the dream
To hope thine aid without the aid of him
Who gave thee birth and taught thee where to flow,
And in thy waves his various blessings show.

May R—— return to view his native shore,
Replete with vigour not his own before – 30
Then shall we see, with pleasure and surprise,
And own thy work, great Ruler of the skies!

TO THE REV. DR THOMAS AMORY

*On Reading His Sermons on Daily Devotion,
in which that Duty is Recommended and Assisted*

To cultivate in ev'ry noble mind
Habitual grace and sentiments refin'd,
Thus while you strive to mend the human heart,
Thus while the heav'nly precepts you impart,

O may each bosom catch the sacred fire,
And youthful minds to Virtue's throne aspire!

When God's eternal ways you set in sight,
And Virtue shines in all her native light,
In vain would Vice her works in night conceal,
For Wisdom's eye pervades the sable veil.   10

Artists may paint the sun's effulgent rays,
But Amory's pen the brighter God displays;
While his great works in Amory's pages shine,
And while he proves his essence all divine,
The atheist sure no more can boast aloud
Of chance, or nature, and exclude the God;
As if the clay without the potter's aid
Should rise in various forms and shapes self-made,
Or worlds above with orb o'er orb profound
Self-mov'd could run the everlasting round.   20
It cannot be – unerring Wisdom guides,
With eye propitious, and o'er all presides.

Still prosper, Amory! still may'st thou receive
The warmest blessings which a muse can give,
And when this transitory state is o'er,
When kingdoms fall, and fleeting Fame's no more,
May Amory triumph in immortal fame –
A nobler title and superior name!

ON THE DEATH OF J.C.

An infant

No more the flow'ry scenes of pleasure rife,
Nor charming prospects greet the mental eyes,
No more with joy we view that lovely face –
Smiling, disportive, flush'd with ev'ry grace.

The tear of sorrow flows from ev'ry eye,
Groans answer groans, and sighs to sighs reply;
What sudden pangs shot thro' each aching heart,
When, Death, thy messenger dispatch'd his dart?
Thy dread attendants, all-destroying pow'r,
Hurried the infant to his mortal hour.   10
Couldst thou unpitying close those radiant eyes?
Or fail'd his artless beauties to surprise?
Could not his innocence thy stroke control,
Thy purpose shake and soften all thy soul?

The blooming babe, with shades of Death o'er-spread,
No more shall smile, no more shall raise its head,
But, like a branch that from the tree is torn,
Falls prostrate, wither'd, languid and forlorn.
'Where flies my James?' 'tis thus I seem to hear
The parent ask; 'Some angel, tell me where   20
He wings his passage thro' the yielding air!'
Methinks a cherub bending from the skies
Observes the question, and serene replies,
'In heav'ns high palaces your babe appears:

Prepare to meet him and dismiss your tears.'
Shall not th'intelligence your grief restrain,
And turn the mournful to the cheerful strain?
Cease your complaints, suspend each rising sigh,
Cease to accuse the Ruler of the sky.
Parents, no more indulge the falling tear: 30
Let Faith to heav'n's refulgent domes repair;
There see your infant, like a seraph glow:
What charms celestial in his numbers flow
Melodious, while the foul-enchanting strain
Dwells on his tongue, and fills th'ethereal plain?
Enough – for ever cease your murm'ring breath;
Not as a foe but friend converse with Death,
Since to the port of happiness unknown
He brought that treasure which you call your own.
The gift of Heav'n, entrusted to your hand, 40
Cheerful resign at the divine command –
Not at your bar must sov'reign Wisdom stand.

A HYMN TO HUMANITY

To S.P.G., Esq.

I

Lo! for this dark terrestrial ball
Forsakes his azure-paved hall
   A prince of heav'nly birth!
Divine humanity behold:
What wonders rise, what charms unfold
   At his descent to earth!

II

The bosoms of the great and good
With wonder and delight he view'd,
    And fix'd his empire there:
Him, close compressing to his breast,   10
The sire of gods and men address'd:
    'My son, my heav'nly fair!

III

'Descend to earth, there place thy throne;
To succour man's afflicted son
    Each human heart inspire:
To act in bounties unconfin'd
Enlarge the close, contracted mind
    And fill it with thy fire.'

IV

Quick as the word, with swift career
He wings his course from star to star   20
    And leaves the bright abode.
The virtue did his charms impart;
Their G——y! then thy raptur'd heart
    Perceiv'd the rushing God:

V

For when thy pitying eye did see
The languid muse in low degree,
    Then, then at thy desire

Descended the celestial nine;
O'er me methought they deign'd to shine,
   And deign'd to string my lyre. 30

VI

Can Afric's muse forgetful prove?
Or can such friendship fail to move
   A tender human heart?
Immortal Friendship laurel-crown'd
The smiling graces all surround
   With ev'ry heav'nly art.

TO THE HONOURABLE T.H., ESQ.

On the Death of His Daughter

While deep you mourn beneath the cypress shade
The hand of Death, and your dear daughter laid
In dust, whose absence gives your tears to flow
And racks your bosom with incessant woe,
Let recollection take a tender part,
Assuage the raging tortures of your heart,
Still the wild tempest of tumultuous grief
And pour the heav'nly nectar of relief:
Suspend the sigh, dear sir, and check the groan –
Divinely bright your daughter's virtues shone: 10
How free from scornful pride her gentle mind,

Which ne'er its aid to indigence declin'd!
Expanding free, it sought the means to prove
Unfailing charity, unbounded love!

She unreluctant flies to see no more
Her dear-lov'd parents on earth's dusky shore:
Impatient heav'n's resplendent goal to gain,
She with swift progress cuts the azure plain,
Where grief subsides, where changes are no more
And life's tumultuous billows cease to roar;   20
She leaves her earthly mansion for the skies,
Where new creations feast her wond'ring eyes.

To heav'n's high mandate cheerfully resign'd
She mounts, and leaves the rolling globe behind;
She, who late wish'd that Leonard might return,
Has ceas'd to languish, and forgot to mourn;
To the same high empyreal mansions come,
She joins her spouse and smiles upon the tomb:
And thus I hear her from the realms above:
'Lo! this the kingdom of celestial love!   30
Could ye, fond parents, see our present bliss,
How soon would you each sigh, each fear dismiss!
Amidst unutter'd pleasures whilst I play
In the fair sunshine of celestial day,
As far as grief affects a happy soul,
So far doth grief my better mind control,
To see on earth my aged parents mourn,
And secret wish for T——l to return;
Let brighter scenes your ev'ning hours employ:
Converse with heav'n and taste the promis'd joy.'   40

NIOBE IN DISTRESS FOR HER CHILDREN

Slain by Apollo, from Ovid's Metamorphoses, *Book VI, and from a View of the Painting of Mr Richard Wilson**

Apollo's wrath to man the dreadful spring
Of ills innum'rous, tuneful goddess, sing!
Thou who did'st first th'ideal pencil give,
And taught'st the painter in his works to live,
Inspire with glowing energy of thought
What Wilson painted and what Ovid wrote.
Muse! lend thy aid, nor let me sue in vain,
Tho' last and meanest of the rhyming train!
O guide my pen in lofty strains to show
The Phrygian queen, all beautiful in woe.   10
    'Twas where Maeonia* spreads her wide domain
Niobe dwelt, and held her potent reign:
See in her hand the regal sceptre shine,
The wealthy heir of Tantalus divine,
He most distinguish'd by Dodonean Jove,*
To approach the tables of the gods above:
Her grandsire Atlas, who with mighty pains
Th'ethereal axis on his neck sustains;
Her other grandsire on the throne on high
Rolls the loud-pealing thunder thro' the sky.*   20

Her spouse, Amphion, who from Jove too springs,
Divinely taught to sweep the sounding strings.

Seven sprightly sons the royal bed adorn,
Seven daughters beauteous as the op'ning morn,
As when Aurora fills the ravish'd sight,
And decks the orient realms with rosy light
From their bright eyes the living splendours play,
Nor can beholders bear the flashing ray.

Wherever, Niobe, thou turn'st thine eyes,
New beauties kindle, and new joys arise! 30
But thou hadst far the happier mother prov'd,
If this fair offspring had been less belov'd:
What if their charms exceed Aurora's taint?
No words could tell them, and no pencil paint,
Thy love too vehement hastens to destroy
Each blooming maid, and each celestial boy.

Now Manto* comes, endu'd with mighty skill,
The past to explore, the future to reveal.
Thro' Thebes' wide streets Tiresia's daughter came,
Divine Latona's* mandate to proclaim: 40
The Theban maids to hear the orders ran,
When thus Maeonia's prophetess began:

'Go, Thebans! Great Latona's will obey,
And pious tribute at her altars pay:
With rights divine, the goddess be implor'd,
Nor be her sacred offspring unador'd.'
Thus Manto spoke. The Theban maids obey,
And pious tribute to the goddess pay.
The rich perfumes ascend in waving spires,
And altars blaze with consecrated fires; 50
The fair assembly moves with graceful air,
And leaves of laurel bind the flowing hair.

   Niobe comes with all her royal race,
With charms unnumber'd and superior grace:
Her Phrygian garments of delightful hue,
Inwove with gold, refulgent to the view,
Beyond description beautiful she moves
Like heav'nly Venus,* 'midst her smiles and loves:
She views around the supplicating train,
And shakes her graceful head with stern disdain;   60
Proudly she turns around her lofty eyes,
And thus reviles celestial deities:
'What madness drives the Theban ladies fair
To give their incense to surrounding air?
Say, why this new-sprung deity preferr'd?
Why vainly fancy your petitions heard?
Or say why Coeus' offspring* is obey'd,
While to my goddeship no tribute's paid?
For me no altars blaze with living fires,
No bullock bleeds, no frankincense transpires –   70
Tho' Cadmus'* palace, not unknown to Fame,
And Phrygian nations all revere my name.
Where'er I turn my eyes vast wealth I find,
Lo! here an empress with a goddess join'd.
What, shall a Titaness be deify'd,
To whom the spacious earth a couch deny'd?
Nor heav'n, nor earth, nor sea receiv'd your queen,
Till pitying Delos* took the wand'rer in.
Round me what a large progeny is spread!
No frowns of fortune has my soul to dread.   80
What if, indignant, she decrease my train?
More than Latona's number will remain;
Then hence, ye Theban dames, hence haste away,

NIOBE IN DISTRESS FOR HER CHILDREN

Nor longer off'rings to Latona pay;
Regard the orders of Amphion's spouse,
And take the leaves of laurel from your brows.'
Niobe spoke. The Theban maids obey'd –
Their brows unbound and left the rights unpaid.

    The angry goddess heard, then silence broke
On Cynthus'* summit, and indignant spoke: 90
'Phoebus! behold, thy mother in disgrace,
Who to no goddess yields the prior place
Except to Juno's* self, who reigns above,
The spouse and sister of the thund'ring Jove.
Niobe, sprung from Tantalus, inspires
Each Theban bosom with rebellious fires;
No reason her imperious temper quells,
But all her father in her tongue rebels;
Wrap her own sons for her blaspheming breath,
Apollo! wrap them in the shades of death.'   100
Latona ceas'd, and ardent thus replies
The God, whose glory decks th'expanded skies.

    'Cease thy complaints – mine be the task assign'd
To punish pride and scourge the rebel mind.'
This Phoebe join'd. They wing their instant flight;
Thebes trembled as th'immortal pow'rs alight.

    With clouds incompass'd glorious Phoebus stands,
The feather'd vengeance quiv'ring in his hands.

    Near Cadmus' walls a plain extended lay,
Where Thebes' young princes pass'd in sport the day: 110
There the bold coursers bounded o'er the plains,
While their great masters held the golden reins.
Ismenus* first the racing pastime led,
And rul'd the fury of his flying steed.

'Ah, me!' he sudden cries, with shrieking breath,
While in his breast he feels the shaft of death;
He drops the bridle on his courser's mane,
Before his eyes in shadows swims the plain,
He, the firstborn of great Amphion's bed,
Was struck the first, first mingled with the dead.   120

    Then didst thou, Sipylus, the language hear
Of fate portentous whistling in the air:
As when th'impending storm the sailor sees,
He spreads his canvas to the fav'ring breeze,
So to thine horse thou gav'st the golden reins,
Gav'st him to rush impetuous o'er the plains:
But ah! a fatal shaft from Phoebus' hand
Smites thro' thy neck, and sinks thee on the sand.

    Two other brothers were at wrestling found,
And in their pastime claspt each other round: 130
A shaft that instant from Apollo's hand
Transfixt them both, and stretcht them on the sand:
Together they their cruel fate bemoan'd,
Together languish'd and together groan'd:
Together too th'unbodied spirits fled,
And sought the gloomy mansions of the dead.

    Alphenor saw, and trembling at the view,
Beat his torn breast, that chang'd its snowy hue.
He flies to raise them in a kind embrace;
A brother's fondness triumphs in his face;   140
Alphenor fails in this fraternal deed –
A dart dispatch'd him (so the fates decreed):
Soon as the arrow left the deadly wound,
His issuing entrails smok'd upon the ground.

    What woes on blooming Damasichon wait!
His sighs portend his near-impending fate.

Just where the well-made leg begins to be,
And the soft sinews form the supple knee,
The youth, sore wounded by the Delian god,*
Attempts t'extract the crime-avenging rod,   150
But whilst he strives the will of fate t'avert,
Divine Apollo sends a second dart;
Swift thro' his throat the feather'd mischief flies,
Bereft of sense, he drops his head and dies.

    Young Ilioneus, the last, directs his pray'r
And cries, 'My life, ye gods celestial, spare!'
Apollo heard, and pity touch'd his heart,
But ah! too late – for he had sent the dart;
Thou too, O Ilioneus, art doom'd to fall –
The fates refuse that arrow to recall.   160

    On the swift wings of ever-flying Fame
To Cadmus' palace soon the tidings came:
Niobe heard, and with indignant eyes
She thus express'd her anger and surprise:
'Why is such privilege to them allow'd?
Why thus insulted by the Delian god?
Dwells there such mischief in the pow'rs above?
Why sleeps the vengeance of immortal Jove?'
For now Amphion, too, with grief oppress'd,
Had plung'd the deadly dagger in his breast.   170
Niobe now, less haughty than before,
With lofty head directs her steps no more.
She, who late told her pedigree divine,
And drove the Thebans from Latona's shrine,
How strangely chang'd! yet beautiful in woe,
She weeps, nor weeps unpity'd by the foe.
On each pale corpse the wretched mother spread

Lay overwhelm'd with grief, and kiss'd her dead,
Then rais'd her arms, and thus, in accents slow:
'Be sated, cruel goddess, with my woe! 180
If I've offended, let these streaming eyes,
And let this sev'nfold funeral suffice:
Ah! take this wretched life you deign'd to save –
With them I too am carried to the grave.
Rejoice triumphant, my victorious foe,
But show the cause from whence your triumphs flow!
Tho' I unhappy mourn these children slain,
Yet greater numbers to my lot remain.'
She ceas'd, the bow string twang'd with awful sound,
Which struck with terror all th'assembly round, 190
Except the queen, who stood unmov'd alone,
By her distresses more presumptuous grown.
Near the pale corpses stood their sisters fair,
In sable vestures and dishevell'd hair;
One, while she draws the fatal shaft away,
Faints, falls and sickens at the light of day.
To soothe her mother, lo! another flies!
And blames the fury of inclement skies,
And, while her words a filial pity show,
Struck dumb – indignant seeks the shades below. 200
Now from the fatal place another flies,
Falls in her flight and languishes and dies.
Another on her sister drops in death;
A fifth in trembling terrors yields her breath;
While the sixth seeks some gloomy cave in vain,
Struck with the rest, and mingled with the slain.
   One only daughter lives, and she the least;
The queen close clasp'd the daughter to her breast:

'Ye heav'nly pow'rs, ah spare me one,' she cry'd.
'Ah! spare me one,' the vocal hills reply'd.   210
In vain she begs – the Fates her suit deny;
In her embrace she sees her daughter die.

   The queen, of all her family bereft,
Without or husband, son or daughter left,
Grew stupid at the shock. The passing air
Made no impression on her stiff'ning hair.
The blood forsook her face: amidst the flood
Pour'd from her cheeks, quite fix'd her eyeballs stood.
Her tongue, her palate both obdurate grew;
Her curdled veins no longer motion knew;   220
The use of neck and arms and feet was gone,
And ev'n her bowels hard'ned into stone:
A marble statue now the queen appears,
But from the marble steal the silent tears.[1]*

TO S.M.,
A YOUNG AFRICAN PAINTER

On Seeing His Works

To show the lab'ring bosom's deep intent,
And thought in living characters to paint,
When first thy pencil did those beauties give,
And breathing figures learnt from thee to live,
How did those prospects give my soul delight,

---

[1] This verse to the end is the work of another hand.

A new creation rushing on my sight?
Still, wond'rous youth! each noble path pursue –
On deathless glories fix thine ardent view:
Still may the painter's and the poet's fire
To aid thy pencil, and thy verse conspire! 10
And may the charms of each seraphic theme
Conduct thy footsteps to immortal fame!
High to the blissful wonders of the skies,
Elate thy soul and raise thy wishful eyes.
Thrice happy, when exalted to survey
That splendid city, crown'd with endless day,
Whose twice six gates on radiant hinges ring:
Celestial Salem blooms in endless spring.

Calm and serene thy moments glide along,
And may the muse inspire each future song! 20
Still, with the sweets of contemplation bless'd,
May peace with balmy wings your soul invest!
But when these shades of time are chas'd away,
And darkness ends in everlasting day,
On what seraphic pinions shall we move,
And view the landscapes in the realms above?
There shall thy tongue in heav'nly murmurs flow,
And there my muse with heav'nly transport glow:
No more to tell of Damon's tender sighs,*
Or rising radiance of Aurora's eyes, 30
For nobler themes demand a nobler strain,
And purer language on th'ethereal plain.
Cease, gentle muse! the solemn gloom of night
Now seals the fair creation from my sight.

TO HIS HONOUR THE LIEUTENANT GOVERNOR

On the Death of His Lady

All-Conquering Death! by thy resistless pow'r,
Hope's tow'ring plumage falls to rise no more!
Of scenes terrestrial how the glories fly –
Forget their splendours, and submit to die!
Who ere escap'd thee, but the saint[1] of old,
Beyond the flood in sacred annals told,
And the great sage,[2] whom fiery coursers drew
To heav'n's bright portals from Elisha's* view;
Wond'ring, he gaz'd at the refulgent car,
Then snatch'd the mantle floating on the air.   10
From death these only could exemption boast,
And without dying gain'd th'immortal coast.
Not falling millions sate the tyrant's mind,
Nor can the victor's progress be confin'd.
But cease thy strife with Death, fond Nature, cease:
He leads the virtuous to the realms of peace;
His to conduct to the immortal plains,
Where heav'n's supreme in bliss and glory reigns.

There sits, illustrious sir, thy beauteous spouse;
A gem-blaz'd circle beaming on her brows.   20

---
[1] Enoch.
[2] Elijah.

Hail'd with acclaim among the heav'nly choirs,
Her soul new-kindling with seraphic fires,
To notes divine she tunes the vocal strings,
While heav'n's high concave with the music rings.
Virtue's rewards can mortal pencil paint?
No – all descriptive arts and eloquence are faint;
Nor canst thou, Oliver, assent refuse
To heav'nly tidings from the Afric muse.

As soon may change thy laws, eternal fate,
As the saint miss the glories I relate; 30
Or her benevolence forgotten lie,
Which wip'd the trick'ling tear from mis'ry's eye.
Whene'er the adverse winds were known to blow,
When loss to loss[1] ensu'd, and woe to woe,
Calm and serene beneath her father's hand
She sat, resign'd to the divine command.

No longer then, great sir, her death deplore,
And let us hear the mournful sigh no more;
Restrain the sorrow streaming from thine eye,
Be all thy future moments crown'd with joy! 40
Nor let thy wishes be to earth confin'd,
But soaring high pursue th'unbodied mind.
Forgive the muse, forgive th'advent'rous lays,
That fain thy soul to heav'nly scenes would raise.

                        24th March, 1773

---

[1] Three amiable daughters who died when just arrived to women's estate.

A FAREWELL TO AMERICA
*To Mrs S. W.**

I

Adieu, New England's smiling meads;
    Adieu, the flow'ry plain –
I leave thine op'ning charms, O spring,
    And tempt the roaring main.

II

In vain for me the flow'rets rise,
    And boast their gaudy pride,
While here beneath the northern skies
    I mourn for health deny'd.

III

Celestial maid of rosy hue,
    O let me feel thy reign!   10
I languish till thy face I view,
    Thy vanish'd joys regain.

IV

Susanna mourns, nor can I bear
    To see the crystal show'r,
Or mark the tender falling tear
    At sad departure's hour;

V

Not unregarding can I see
   Her soul with grief opprest:
But let no sighs, no groans for me,
   Steal from her pensive breast. 20

VI

In vain the feather'd warblers sing;
   In vain the garden blooms;
And on the bosom of the spring
   Breathes out her sweet perfumes.

VII

While for Britannia's distant shore
   We sweep the liquid plain,
And with astonish'd eyes explore
   The wide-extended main.

VIII

Lo! health appears! celestial dame!
   Complacent and serene, 30
With Hebe's mantle* o'er her frame,
   With soul-delighting mien.

IX

To mark the vale where London lies
   With misty vapours crown'd,
Which cloud Aurora's thousand dyes,
   And veil her charms around.

X

Why, Phoebus, moves thy car so slow?
    So slow thy rising ray?
Give us the famous town to view,
    Thou glorious king of day!   40

XI

For thee, Britannia, I resign
    New England's smiling fields;
To view again her charms divine,
    What joy the prospect yields!

XII

But thou! temptation hence away,
    With all thy fatal train,
Nor once seduce my soul away,
    By thine enchanting strain.

XIII

Thrice happy they, whose heav'nly shield
    Secures their souls from harms,   50
And fell temptation on the field
    Of all its pow'r disarms!

                Boston, 7th May, 1773.

A REBUS, BY I.B.*

I

A bird delicious to the taste,
On which an army once did feast,
   Sent by a hand unseen;
A creature of the horned race,
Which Britain's royal standards grace;
   A gem of vivid green;

II

A town of gaiety and sport,
Where beaux and beauteous nymphs resort,
   And gallantry doth reign;
A Dardan hero* fam'd of old
For youth and beauty, as we're told,
   And by a monarch slain;

III

A peer of popular applause,
Who doth our violated laws
   And grievances proclaim.
Th'initials show a vanquish'd town,
That adds fresh glory and renown
   To old Britannia's fame.

AN ANSWER TO THE REBUS

By the Author of these Poems

The poet asks, and Phillis can't refuse
To show th'obedience of the infant muse.
She knows the Quail of most inviting taste
Fed Israel's army in the dreary waste;
And what's on Britain's royal standard borne,
But the tall, graceful, rampant Unicorn?
The Emerald with a vivid verdure glows
Among the gems which regal crowns compose;
Boston's a town, polite and debonair,
To which the beaux and beauteous nymphs repair;
Each Helen* strikes the mind with sweet surprise,
While living lightning flashes from her eyes,
See young Euphorbus of the Dardan line
By Manelaus' hand to death resign;*
The well-known peer of popular applause
Is C——m zealous to support our laws.
   Quebec* now vanquish'd must obey –
She too much annual tribute pay
To Britain of immortal fame,
And add new glory to her name.

FINIS

A MEMOIR OF
PHILLIS WHEATLEY

A Native African and a Slave

NOT A GREAT MANY of the younger readers of this little book* may know much about slavery, though they have all heard and read, of course, that such a thing exists, and that even in the southern and western parts of our own country. I do not intend here to discuss the nature of it, or the circumstances that gave rise to it in the first instance, or the effect it is believed to have on the country and the people in and among which it is found. All these matters are more proper for another place. My object is simply to call the attention of those who feel an interest in the condition and character of the African race to some particulars respecting individuals of that race, who have, at different times, been slaves in different parts of this country, and whose characters were quite too interesting to be passed over by the historian in utter silence.

Of these, the most remarkable is Phillis Wheatley, as she has been commonly called. What her African name was never has been ascertained, for she was but about seven years old when she was brought in a slave ship with many other slaves from that country to this. The vessel in which she came sailed into Boston harbour in the year 1761 – that is, seventy-three years ago. Soon afterwards, the whole 'cargo', as the language was in those times, was offered for sale, and no doubt advertised in the Boston newspapers – for any of my readers who may happen in the course of their lives to look up the Boston papers of that day will find almost all of them, from week to week, more or less filled with advertisements of slaves: sometimes singly and sometimes in 'lots'; sometimes naming them and sometimes not; to be sold, perhaps, or wanted to buy, or to be given away, or run away – in a word, advertisements in all forms, much as they appear nowadays wherever slavery exists, and very much as they appear in the Boston papers of these times respecting cattle and sheep. I have seen, in one of the old Boston papers of 1764, which is now before me as I write, a 'likely Negro boy', published in this way to be sold – in the same advertisement with 'a black moose, about three months old.' Here is another, which I copy from the same paper:

> Cesar, a Negro fellow, noted in town by having no legs, is supposed to be strolling about the country. If he can be brought to the printers for one dollar, besides necessary expenses, it shall be paid.

One gentleman in the same paper informs his customers and the public that he has just opened his goods for sale in Cornhill, near the Post Office, where he will sell them hardware, by wholesale and retail, for ready money; and then he goes on to say that 'a good price will be given for a likely

Negro boy, from 16 to 20 years of age, if he can be well recommended.'

It was not many years after this, however, that slavery came to an end in Massachusetts.* The last I have heard of it from any of the old people who lived in those times is a story which an aged gentleman told me, a few days since, of his going, in the year 1777 (two years after the Revolutionary War* commenced) from Andover, in this state, to Haverhill. He passed by a small house near the roadside, where he saw several black children, male and female, playing in the sunshine near the doorway. They were healthy and happy-looking children, though rather poorly clad and without shoes on, but one of them – a girl, about thirteen years old – struck the fancy of the gentleman, who stopped his horse to look at them, as likely to make very good 'help' for his wife in Cambridge. He knocked at the door and a woman, who appeared to be the mother of the family, came out. He entered into a conversation with her respecting the child with which he was best pleased, and proposed to purchase her. The mother made no objection, except on the score of the price, and this did not continue long, for she soon agreed to sell her daughter for eight dollars – to be given up whenever the gentleman, after consulting his wife about the purchase, should choose to send for her. He went home, and there the matter rested, for his wife had become tired of slaves, and she induced him to give up the bargain.

I mention this incident to remind my readers how short a time it is, comparatively, since respectable people in Massachusetts – where we now boast so much of our freedom and our regard for the equal rights of all men – were concerned in this business of buying and selling the African like so many cattle in the stalls of a cattle show. We have abundant reason to be grateful to a merciful Providence that, while many other sections of our own country, as well as others, are to this day afflicted with the evils of slavery, we are, as we think, much more pleasantly situated. Neither are there now any slaves in Vermont, Maine or New Hampshire, and there are very few, indeed, in Rhode Island and Connecticut – less than a hundred in both those states. In Indiana and Illinois they have none. In Ohio there never were any; and the number still remaining in Pennsylvania, New York, Delaware and New Jersey is quite small.

To return to our little African: she was found out and purchased soon after the advertisement of her appeared (in 1761) by Mrs Wheatley, the wife of Mr John Wheatley, a highly respectable citizen of Boston. This lady is another instance to show that it had not yet become altogether disgraceful among decent people to buy and sell their fellow men in the market to serve their convenience. Mrs Wheatley had several slaves already – acting, as they generally did in Massachusetts, as house servants – but these were getting rather advanced in life, and she wished to obtain one more, active and docile, whom she could herself educate in such a manner as to make her a suitable companion for herself in her old age. It is very evident, such being the good lady's feelings, that the little slave could not have fallen into better hands, if she must be sold. Mrs Wheatley, on the other hand, was much pleased with the appearance of the child, though the poor thing had nothing to recommend it to her notice, or to anybody's, but the meekness and modesty of her manners and her intelligent and comely features. Her only garment at this time was a piece of dirty carpet placed around her, like what is called a 'filibeg'.* The lady preferred her, nevertheless, to the older females, whom she found her with, and, having paid her master the price agreed on, conveyed the half-clad stranger home with herself in a chaise.

At this period she is supposed, as I said before, to have been about seven years old, being in the act of shedding her front teeth. How much of the English language she could speak does not appear* – probably not a great deal, nor with much ease, for she had enjoyed no opportunity of learning it that we hear of, excepting the very limited one she must have had, if she had any, in the course of her passage from the shores of Africa to those of this country, and the little stay she made with her master and her fellow slaves after that time and previous to her being purchased by Mrs Wheatley. Very likely it is owing to this circumstance – her inability to speak the language with much ease or clearness – that we hear scarcely anything of her early history in Africa. It has never been known what part of that continent she came from, to what tribe or kingdom she belonged, what relatives or friends she left behind or sailed with, and everything else of that kind is equally a matter of uncertainty. No doubt, before she had learned enough of the English language to tell her humble history to her new friends – or so much of it as she then remembered – she forgot that little, and very soon found, in the midst of new society, and in a country full of strange sights and sounds, that her mind had become filled with a multitude of new impressions which rapidly crowded out the old.

The little girl who had now received the name by which she has been since known, Phillis Wheatley, being taken into the family of her mistress and treated with exemplary kindness, soon began to show very plain indications of the character and talent which a few years after became so decided and so distinguished. Mrs Wheatley's daughter undertook to teach her writing and reading, and the little girl's disposition to imitate what she had seen in others, in regard to the former of these accomplishments, had already made itself manifest in her childish endeavours to describe letters and figures of different kinds on some of the walls about the house, and upon other stationary of like sort, with a piece of chalk or charcoal. She was not at this time left to associate much with the other servants or slaves of her own colour or condition in the dwelling of her mistress, but was kept almost constantly about her person.

I remarked that nothing of the early history of Phillis could be gathered from her lips. One circumstance alone, it might have been said, she remembered, and that was her mother's custom of 'pouring out water before the sun at his rising'. This, no doubt, was a custom of the tribe to which she belonged, and was one of their religious rites.* That the child should retain the memory of this apparently trifling incident when she forgot almost everything else is not, perhaps, very remarkable. It is one which would be quite as likely to make an impression on the mind of a child as a much more important event. One writer, who has treated of the life of Phillis,* says in relation to this subject, very properly: 'We cannot know at how early a period she was beguiled from the hut of her mother, or how long a time elapsed between her abduction from her first home and her being transferred to the abode of her benevolent mistress, where she must have felt like one awaking from a fearful dream. This interval was, no doubt, a long one, and filled, as it must have been, with various degrees and kinds of suffering, might naturally enough obliterate the recollection of earlier and happier days. The solitary exception which held its place so tenaciously in her mind was probably renewed from day to day through this long season of affliction, for, every morning, when the bereaved child saw the sun emerging from the wide waters, she must have thought of her mother prostrating herself before the first golden beam that glanced across her native plains.'

The opportunities of learning became greater to Phillis as she advanced in life. Her friends, who had already taken a deep interest in her improvement, were encouraged, both by the rapid advances she made and the warm gratitude which their efforts excited, to increased exertions in her favour. She had begun also to attract the attention of the society of the city, out of the family of her mistress, and, as the fame of her talent and virtue extended itself, she received favours from several of the literary characters of the day, in the shape of books and other aids to her education. Her own desire of knowledge increased, as such desire generally does, with every gratification. She made considerable progress in belles-lettres,* and then she acquainted herself, in a good degree, with the Latin tongue – evidence of which acquirements may be frequently observed in her poems.

Of the place she had, by this time – in consequence of her amiable traits of character, no less than of her extraordinary intellectual exhibition – obtained in the family, and especially in the affection of her excellent mistress, some idea may be formed from the following incident, which is referred to by the writer I have already borrowed from.

It is related that, upon the occasion of one of the visits she was invited to pay to her neighbours, the weather changed during the absence of Phillis, and her anxious mistress, fearful of the effects of cold and damp upon her already delicate health, ordered Prince (also an African and a slave) to take the chaise and bring home her protegée. When the chaise returned, the good lady drew near the window as it approached the house, and exclaimed: 'Do but look at the saucy varlet – if he hasn't the impudence to sit upon the same seat with my Phillis!' and poor Prince received a severe reprimand for forgetting the dignity thus kindly, though perhaps to him unaccountably, attached to the sable person of 'my Phillis'.[1]

The prejudice, so common in those times against coloured people, even more than now, which this anecdote indicates in the mind of Mrs Wheatley may be readily pardoned for the sake of the kindness which the good lady manifested in favour of the more fortunate servant of the two.

It would have been no very wonderful thing, under these circumstances of partiality, and perhaps sometimes flattery, if the mind of the young favourite had been influenced more than it should be by the compliments she constantly received. That it was not so influenced, so far as we can ascertain, and that, on the contrary, she can scarcely be said to have known – or, at least, to have shown – what pride and vanity were is a circumstance highly indicative of the excellent good sense which was among her most obvious natural endowments. It is said that when, as I have already

---

[1] See 'Memoir' prefixed to the *Poems* lately republished in Boston.

intimated was often the case, she was invited, with or without the other members of the family of Mrs Wheatley, to visit individuals of wealth and distinction, she always declined the seat offered her at their board, and, requesting that a side-table might be laid for her, dined modestly apart from the rest of the company. This was, no doubt, the wisest, as well as most modest, course she could take. However illiberal and unchristian might be the prejudice, which many people entertained in those days, and which many are not rid of, against their fellow citizens – or at least fellow *men* – who are 'guilty of a skin not coloured like their own',* it was peculiarly amiable in Phillis to be content, according to the admonition of the holy apostle, with the condition wherein she was placed by Providence; and it was equally prudent in her not to increase the evils of that condition by permitting such trifles, as they must have appeared to a mind like hers, to make her unhappy for a single moment. Her modesty admirably contrasted with her merit, and powerfully increased its charms.

The earliest attempt in poetical composition by Phillis which has been preserved – though she probably made many at an earlier date – is the little poem intended to express her loyal acknowledgements to the King (George III), on occasion of the Repeal of the Stamp Act – an event of intense interest in all the American Colonies. It shows a degree of grammatical correctness and a propriety of sentiment and feeling which certainly do not disgrace the literary character of a slave at the age of fourteen years – for the piece was written in 1768. It is as follows:

Your subjects hope, dread sire,
The crown upon your brows may flourish long,
And that your arm may in your God be strong!
O may your sceptre num'rous nations sway,
And all with love and readiness obey!

But how shall we the British King reward?
Rule thou in peace, our father and our lord!
Midst the remembrance of thy favours past,
The meanest peasants most admire the last.
May George, beloved by all the nations round,
Live with Heav'n's choicest constant blessings crown'd!
Great God, direct and guard him from on high,
And from his head let ev'ry evil fly!
And may each clime with equal gladness see
A monarch's smile can set his subjects free!

In the year 1769 or 1770, Phillis was received as a member of the church worshipping in the Old South Meeting House, which for several years while she attended there was under the pastoral charge of the excellent Dr Sewell. He died in 1769, and the following poem, written by Phillis on that occasion, will sufficiently illustrate both the character of the subject and the feelings with which the amiable author regarded that melancholy event. It shows also an evident improvement in her style:

Ere yet the morn its lovely blushes spread,
See Sewell number'd with the happy dead.
Hail, holy man, arriv'd th'immortal shore,
Though we shall hear thy warning voice no more.

Come, let us all behold with wishful eyes
The saint ascending to his native skies;
From hence the prophet wing'd his rapt'rous way
To the blest mansions in eternal day.
Then, begging for the Spirit of our God,
And panting eager for the same abode,   10
Come, let us all with the same vigour rise,
And take a prospect of the blissful skies;
While on our minds Christ's image is imprest,
And the dear Saviour glows in ev'ry breast.
Thrice happy saint! to find thy heav'n at last –
What compensation for the evils past!

Great God, incomprehensible, unknown,
By sense, we bow at thine exalted throne.
O, while we beg thine excellence to feel,
Thy sacred Spirit to our hearts reveal,   20
And give us of that mercy to partake,
Which thou hast promis'd for the Saviour's sake!

'Sewell is dead!' swift-pinion'd Fame thus cry'd.
'Is Sewell dead?' my trembling tongue reply'd.
O, what a blessing in his flight deny'd!
How oft for us the holy prophet pray'd!
How oft to us the word of Life convey'd!
By duty urg'd my mournful verse to close,
I for his tomb this epitaph compose:

'Lo, here a man, redeem'd by Jesus' blood,   30
A sinner once, but now a saint with God;
Behold ye rich, ye poor, ye fools, ye wise,

Not let his monument your heart surprise;
'Twill tell you what this holy man has done,
Which gives him brighter lustre than the sun.
Listen, ye happy, from your seats above!
I speak sincerely, while I speak and love;
He fought the paths of piety and truth,
By these made happy from his early youth;
In blooming years that grace divine he felt,   40
Which rescues sinners from the chains of guilt.
Mourn him, ye indigent, whom he has fed,
And henceforth seek, like him, for living bread;
Ev'n Christ, the bread descending from above,
And ask an int'rest in his saving love.
Mourn him, ye youth, to whom he oft has told
God's gracious wonders from the times of old.
I too have cause this mighty loss to mourn,
For he my monitor will not return.
O, when shall we to his blest state arrive?   50
When the same graces in our bosoms thrive.'

Since we are making extracts from these exceedingly interesting compositions – the poems of a slave – we will add another, written the next year after the last – that is, in 1770 – on occasion of the decease of the Rev. Mr Whitefield, the celebrated Methodist clergyman, an eminently distinguished man in his time, and whose memory is even to this day much cherished by many persons of advanced age, who listened to his eloquent exhortations from the Boston pulpits and the Boston Common. Vast multitudes of hearers thronged around him wherever he preached in England (which was his native land), or in this country, and great numbers of these were impressed by his appeal to their consciences and hearts, as Phillis seems to have been, in a manner which they never afterwards could forget. She alludes with great propriety, as it will be seen, 'to the music of his tongue', for his voice was one of the most agreeable and powerful with which a public speaker was ever gifted. She says, too, very beautifully,

> Thou moon hast seen, and all the stars of light,
> How he has wrestled with his god by night,

referring to those frequent occasions on which the devoted clergyman had retired to the fields and woods in the solitude of midnight, as well as amid the glare of the noonday, to commune on his knees with that Being, to the advancement of whose kingdom on earth he consecrated the energies of his body and his mind. Mr Whitefield died during one of his numerous visits to this country, at Newburyport, where his grave, with the inscription on the marble, may still be seen.

> Hail, happy saint, on thine immortal throne,
> Possest of glory, life and bliss unknown;
> We hear no more the music of thy tongue;
> Thy wonted auditories cease to throng.
> Thy sermons in unequall'd accents flow'd,
> And ev'ry bosom with devotion glow'd;
> Thou didst in strains of eloquence refin'd
> Inflame the heart and captivate the mind.
> Unhappy we the setting sun deplore –
> So glorious once, but ah! it shines no more.   10

Behold the prophet in his tow'ring flight!
He leaves the earth for heav'n's unmeasur'd height,
And worlds unknown receive him from our sight.
There Whitefield wings with rapid course his way,
And sails to Zion through vast seas of day.
Thy pray'rs, great saint, and thine incessant cries
Have pierc'd the bosom of thy native skies.
Thou moon hast seen, and all the stars of light,
How he has wrestled with his god by night.
He pray'd that grace in ev'ry heart might dwell; 20
He long'd to see America excel;
He charg'd its youth that ev'ry grace divine
Should with full lustre in their conduct shine;
That Saviour, which his soul did first receive
The greatest gift that ev'n a god can give,
He freely offer'd to the num'rous throng
That on his lips with list'ning pleasure hung.

'Take him, ye wretched, for your only good;
Take him ye starving sinners, for your food;
Ye thirsty, come to this life-giving stream; 30
Ye preachers, take him for your joyful theme;
Take him, my dear Americans, he said;
Be your complaints on his kind bosom laid;
Take him, ye Africans, he longs for you;
Impartial Saviour is his title due;
Wash'd in the fountain of redeeming blood,
You shall be sons and kings and priests to God.'

Great Countess, we Americans revere
Thy name, and mingle in thy grief sincere;

> New England deeply feels, the orphans mourn,   40
> Their more-than-father will no more return.
>
> But, though arrested by the hand of death,
> Whitefield no more exerts his lab'ring breath,
> Yet let us view him in th'eternal skies;
> Let ev'ry heart to this bright vision rise;
> While the tomb safe retains its sacred trust,
> Till life divine reanimates his dust.

Of the excellent kindness of feeling, as well as talent and propriety of sentiment, which is manifested in these poems, I need not speak. It is time, however, to call the attention of my readers to the sequel of the history of the authoress.

Her constitution was always frail, and her health at no time firm. Early in 1773, it became decidedly worse than it had been before, and so much so that her fond friends, and especially Mrs Wheatley, became alarmed on her account. Her physician recommended a sea voyage, and, this according with the opinion of the family who were most interested in her welfare, she was induced to avail herself of the opportunity of visiting England, offered her by the departure of a son of her mistress, who was about sailing on a mercantile engagement. She went with him in the summer of the same year, being now about nineteen years of age. The writer of the notice to which I have before referred has the following remarks in reference to this short but interesting visit:

Phillis was well received in England, and was presented to Lady Huntingdon, Lord Dartmouth and many other individuals of distinction; but, says our informant, 'not all the attention she received, nor all the honours that were heaped upon her, had the slightest influence upon her temper or deportment. She was still the same single-hearted, unsophisticated being.' During her stay in England, her poems were given to the world, dedicated to the Countess of Huntingdon and embellished with an engraving, which is said to have been a striking representation of the original.* It is supposed that one of these impressions was forwarded to her mistress as soon as they were struck off, for a grand-niece of Mrs Wheatley's informs us that, during the absence of Phillis, she one day called upon her relative, who immediately directed her attention to a picture over the fireplace, exclaiming: 'See! Look at my Phillis! Does she not seem as though she would speak to me!'

Phillis arrived in London so late in the season that the great market of fashion was deserted. She was therefore urgently pressed by her distinguished friends to remain until the Court returned to St James's, that she might be presented to the young monarch, George III. She would probably have consented to this arrangement, had not letters from America informed her of the declining health of her mistress, who entreated her to return, that she might once more behold her beloved protegée.

Phillis waited not a second bidding, but immediately re-embarked, and arrived in safety at that once-happy home, which was so soon to be desolate.

Mrs Wheatley died in 1774, and her husband and daughter not long afterwards, leaving our African orphan once more almost desolate. After spending a short time with one of the friends of Mrs Wheatley, she now took an apartment and lived alone. The Revolution was at this period fast coming on, and the general discouragement and distress which it brought with it were already beginning to be felt among all classes. Phillis, no doubt, must have borne – though in silent fortitude – her share of the troubles of the times.

At this period of destitution, Phillis received an offer of marriage from a respectable coloured man of Boston, named Peters, who kept a grocery in Court Street and was a man of very handsome person and manners (as our writer informs us), wore a wig, carried a cane and quite acted out 'the gentleman'. In an evil hour he was accepted; and he proved utterly unworthy of the distinguished woman who honoured him by her alliance. He was unsuccessful in business, and failed soon after their marriage; and, though an intelligent man, he is said to have been both too proud and too indolent to apply himself to any occupation below his fancied dignity. Hence his unfortunate wife suffered much from this ill-omened union.

After the Revolution broke out, and Boston was besieged by the enemy, the distress which I have before alluded to very much increased, and multitudes of the inhabitants took the earliest opportunity to find an asylum somewhere in the country towns. Phillis accompanied her husband to Wilmington, and lived there several years, during which we hear scarcely anything of her, excepting that she became the mother of three children, in as many years, of whose subsequent history still less has been ascertained. Some time after the evacuation of the city, she returned, and there resided several weeks with a niece of Mrs Wheatley's, a widow of considerable wealth. During this period, Phillis, who seems to have exerted herself to the utmost to make the best of her circumstances, taught a small day school, and at the end of it, her husband having also come in from the country and reclaimed her society, she and her little family accompanied him to the lodgings he had provided in town.

From this date we learn but little of her, and it may reasonably be inferred from this circumstance, as well as from the general state of those times, that she partook largely of the suffering which pervaded the whole community, and particularly its poorer classes.

In noticing this condition of things, the writer of the latest memoir of Phillis has the following just remarks:

The depreciation of the currency added greatly to the general distress. Mr Thacher, for example, in his *History of Plymouth*,* tells us of a man who sold a cow for forty dollars and gave the same sum for a goose! We have ourselves heard an elderly lady relate that her husband, serving in the army, forwarded her in a letter fifty dollars, which was of so little value when she received it that she paid the whole for a quarter of mutton so poor and so tough that it required great skill and patience in the culinary department to render it fit for the table. 'In this condition of things,' observes the lady, whom we have more than once referred to, and to whom we expressed our surprise at the neglect and poverty into which Phillis was suffered to decline, 'people had other things to attend to than prose and poetry, and had little to bestow in charity when their own children were clamorous for bread.' Poor Phillis was left to the care of her negligent husband.

I may take this occasion to add to the above illustration of the worth of the 'Continental Money' the fact, which I have heard from an old gentleman, that he once paid between ten and eleven hundred dollars in that currency for a tolerable load of wood, and I believe he thought himself doing pretty well by the bargain!

The close of the history of Phillis is even sadder than any of its previous pages. She died in the year 1780, having lost two of her children, and suffered in her own person the united pains of sickness, privation, exposure and fatigue, to an extent which is melancholy to contemplate even for a moment. No stone now tells the stranger where rest the ashes of the Boston Slave of the Revolution.*

Yet she is not forgotten. The character of Phillis is too remarkable, and her brief career too extraordinary, to be overlooked by the friends of virtue or the admirers of genius. Her memory will be cherished, in many a benevolent heart, long after the proud names of those who perhaps despised her, and her humble merits alike shall be buried in the dust of oblivion.

If any reader has, perchance, in the perusal of this slight tribute to her worth, felt the idea suggesting itself to his prejudice that the country or the complexion of the subject of my memoir might have been a sufficient reason for omitting to notice her at all, I cannot, perhaps, make a more suitable admonition to such a mind than in the language of her own:

> 'Twas mercy brought me from my pagan land,
> Taught my benighted soul to understand
> That there's a God – that there's a Saviour too;
> Once I redemption neither fought nor knew;
> Some view our sable race with scornful eye:
> 'Their colour is a diabolic dye!'
> Remember, Christians: Negroes, black as Cain,
> May be refin'd, and join th'angelic train.

In regard to the poetry of Phillis, it will be observed by those who examine her works that she has written almost wholly upon occasional subjects, apparently on those of mere feeling, suggested to her by the occurrence of some event in which her own sympathies were deeply interested. The subjects, accordingly, are quite as illustrative of her own heart and mind as the style is. When this circumstance is considered, in connection with the fact that she was born and brought up to her eighth year a complete barbarian in a barbarous land; that at that period she was made a slave, that in this condition and at this age she commenced the business of self-education, that she had to contend through life with all these circumstances, added to the prejudice commonly entertained against persons of her colour, and much of the time, too, with its most trying personal sufferings – it must be admitted that her compositions furnish abundant proof of a degree of native genius which is exceedingly rare among persons of any race, class or condition. Some of them show also that she had contrived, by some means, not only to make herself familiar with the Holy Scriptures, which seem to have been her favourite authority and study, but to have read and remembered not a little of ancient and modern profane history, geography, astronomy, poetry and other matters of the kind, of which in her times it was considered no disgrace, certainly, for ladies (not to say gentlemen) of a much higher standing in society, to be much more uninformed. Few of them, we presume, would have been unwilling to acknowledge their claims to the following, had they written it – the first lines of an address to the Earl of Dartmouth, a leading English statesman (under George III), to whom Phillis was introduced in that country:

> Hail, happy day, when, smiling like the morn,
> Fair Freedom rose New England to adorn:
> The northern clime beneath her genial ray,
> Dartmouth, congratulates thy blissful sway:
> Elate with hope her race no longer mourns;
> Each soul expands, each grateful bosom burns;
> While in thine hand with pleasure we behold
> The silken reins, and Freedom's charms unfold.
> Long lost to realms beneath the northern skies
> She shines supreme, while hated faction dies: 10
> Soon as appear'd the goddess long desir'd,
> Sick at the view, she languish'd and expir'd;
> Thus from the splendours of the morning light
> The owl in sadness seeks the caves of night.

We will conclude our extracts from these poems (the whole of which have been recently republished in one small volume) with the lines addressed to Harvard University at Cambridge, which, it will be seen, contain an allusion to the early history of the authoress, plainly indicative of the feeling with which she recalled so much as she knew of it:

> While an intrinsic ardour prompts to write,
> The muses promise to assist my pen;
> 'Twas not long since I left my native shore –
> The land of errors and Egyptian gloom;
> Father of mercy, 'twas thy gracious hand
> Brought me in safety from those dark abodes.
>
> Students, to you 'tis giv'n to scan the heights
> Above, to traverse the ethereal space,
> And mark the systems of revolving worlds.
> Still more, ye sons of science, ye receive   10
> The blissful news by messengers from heav'n,
> How Jesus' blood for your redemption flows.
> See him with hands outstretcht upon the cross;
> Immense compassion in his bosom glows;
> He hears revilers, nor resents their scorn:
> What matchless mercy in the Son of God!
> When the whole human race by sin had fall'n,
> He deign'd to die that they might rise again
> And share with him, in the sublimest skies,
> Life without death, and glory without end.   20
>
> Improve your privileges while they stay,
> Ye pupils, and each hour redeem, that bears
> Or good or bad report of you to heav'n.
> Let sin, that baneful evil to the soul,
> By you be shunn'd, nor once remit your guard;

> Suppress the deadly serpent in its egg.
> Ye blooming plants of human race divine,
> An Ethiop tells you 'tis your greatest foe;
> Its transient sweetness turns to endless pain,
> And in immense perdition sinks the soul.   30

Several reflections are suggested by the facts of the preceding memoir, too obvious to be overlooked by any reader who is willing to derive benefit or pleasure from even the humblest source.

One is that genius is not limited by the Creator of man to any colour, country or condition. The darkest skin may cover the brightest intellect, as well as the warmest heart. This consideration should serve to allay that ungenerous contempt which is still but too commonly entertained, unworthy as it is of a liberal mind, towards a class of our fellow men whose chief fault it seems to be that they have been made, in their ignorance and heathenism, the victims of the avarice of the civilised world.

Another is that determination and perseverance, under favour of Providence, are sufficient to accomplish almost anything. Phillis has immortalised herself by her poems; and yet she commenced her literary career a savage and slave, ignorant of the merest rudiments of the language in which she afterwards wrote, and for some time using, in her awkward efforts to give vent to her rising conceptions, no better materials than charcoal or a piece of chalk! Surely no man, woman or child, in whatever circumstances, has occasion after this to be discouraged in an honest exertion to add to his own usefulness and the happiness of the world around. The lowliest being that lives – let him but rely meekly on God's blessing, and upon his own best use of the faculties which that good Being has given him – need not despair of doing something to render the memory of his name precious to some one heart, at least, that shall mourn for him long after the frail remains of his mortal body shall be mixed with the common dust from which it sprung. If any reader of mine, then, shall ever give way for a moment to a feeling of despondence, or of distrust of the goodness of an overruling Providence, let me advise him to think of the poor Boston Slave, and murmur and doubt no more.

NOTE ON THE TEXT

The text of this edition is based on two texts: the first part – the poems – is based on the first edition of *Poems on Various Subjects, Religious and Moral by Phillis Wheatley, Negro Servant to Mr John Wheatley, of Boston, in New England*, which was published in London in 1773 by Archibald Bell. Although various editions of the poems were subsequently published, this edition is widely considered to be the authoritative text, since it is the only edition Wheatley is known to have been directly involved in the preparation of. Where dates of composition were provided in the original publication (largely reflecting the events described) they are given after the relevant poem.

The second part of this volume is based on the first edition of *Memoir of Phillis Wheatley: A Native African and a Slave* by Benjamin Bussey ('B.B.') Thatcher (1809–40), which was first published by George W. Light in Boston in 1834.

The final part of this edition – the Appendix – takes its text from the same two texts: *Poems on Various Subjects* and the *Memoir* both carried a notice 'To the Public', and the *Poems* contained a preface. (See the present edition's note 'To the Public', on p. 9, for more information.)

The spelling, punctuation and grammar have been silently corrected in order to make the text more appealing to the modern reader. The footnotes to the poems are Wheatley's own, and to the memoir Thatcher's own.

NOTES

NOTES TO THE POEMS

13   *Maecenas*: Gaius Maecenas (*c*.70 BC–8 BC) was a Roman statesman, adviser of Augustus and patron of poets, including Horace and Virgil.

13   *Patroclus... Achilles*: A reference to two central characters from Homer's *Iliad*.

13   *Pelides*: Another name for Achilles.

13   *The nine*: The nine muses in Greek and Roman mythology.

13   *Great Maro... glows*: A reference to Virgil's *Miscellanies*: 'Great Maro's breast receiv'd the heav'nly dreams'.

13   *Mantuan sage*: Virgil is traditionally thought to have been born in the village of Andes (now Virgilio, in Lombardy) near Mantua.

14   *Helicon*: Mount Helicon, a mountain in Greece, was believed by the ancient Greeks to be the home of the muses.

14   *Terence... inspir'd*: Publius Terentius Afer (*c*.190–*c*.159 BC) was a Roman playwright. He was brought to Rome as a slave by senator Terentius Lucanus, who educated him and, impressed by his abilities, freed him.

14   *naiads... repose*: Naiads are river-dwelling nymphs in classical mythology.

14   *Phoebus*: A reference to Apollo, the god of the sun.

14   *Aurora*: A reference to the Roman goddess of the dawn.

14   *Parnassus*: Mount Parnassus, a mountain in Greece, was associated with Apollo and the muses by the ancient Greeks, and was a symbol of poetry.

16   *the University of Cambridge in New England*: A reference to Harvard University, which is in Cambridge, Massachusetts.

17   *Ethiop*: Both 'Egyptian' and 'Ethiop' were commonly used to describe someone from Africa, irrespective of where in Africa they were from.

17   *Midst the remembrance... the last*: The Stamp Act of 1765 was an Act of Parliament that imposed a tax on printed materials in the British

colonies in America. There was great resistance to the Stamp Act, and it was officially repealed by King George III (1738–1820) in March 1766.
18 *Cain*: In the Bible, Cain was the eldest son of Adam and Eve, who murdered his brother, Abel.
21 *Zion*: The Promised Land; heaven.
26 *Gath*: Gath was a Philistine city state.
26 *The greaves… prest*: Greaves were pieces of armour that covered the shin; 'targe' is an archaic term for a shield.
27 *Jacob's race*: Jacob, later known as Israel, was a Hebrew patriarch, and is important in all Abrahamic religions; his name was synonymous with the Israelites.
27 *Philistia*: The area occupied by the Philistines.
27 *Jesse's son*: Jesse, or Yishai, was the father of David, who later became King of the Israelites.
28 *Eliab*: Eliab was Jesse's eldest son, and therefore David's older brother.
32 *Saul*: The first King of Israel.
32 *Salem*: The Biblical name for Jerusalem.
32 *son of Ner*: Abner, the son of Ner and cousin of Saul, was the commander of Saul's army.
34 *Sol*: The sun in Roman mythology, often referred to as a god.
41 *Calliope*: The muse of eloquence and epic poetry.
43 *Idumea's… Bozrah's*: Idumea was an adjacent territory to the ancient kingdom of Edom, but in many classical texts it is used to refer to Edom itself – an area which is split between modern Israel and Jordan. Bozrah ('sheepfold' in Hebrew) was the capital city of Edom.
44 *Mneme*: One of the three original (Boeotian) muses – not one of the nine Olympian muses (see fourth note to p. 13) – Mneme was the muse of memory, or recollection.
44 *Phoebe's… regent of the night*: Phoebe, or Selene, was the ancient Greek goddess of the moon.
47 *Sylvanus*: Sylvanus was the Roman god of the woods.
47 *Tithon's*: Tithonus was a prince of Troy and the lover of Eos, the goddess of the dawn (the Greek equivalent of the Roman goddess Aurora).

50 *William, Earl of Dartmouth*: This poem is addressed to William Legge, 2nd Earl of Dartmouth (1731–1801), who was Secretary of State for the Colonies.

52 *Neptune*: The Roman god of the sea.

52 *Aeolus's… roar*: Aeolus was the ancient Greek keeper of the winds.

52 *My Susanna*: A reference to Susanna Wheatley, Phillis' mistress, named in the subtitle of the poem; see also 'A Farewell to America' on p. 79, which is addressed to Susanna.

55 *Boreas*: Boreas was the ancient Greek god of the north wind.

55 *Nereids*: Nereids were sea nymphs in Greek mythology.

59 *Aesculapius*: The ancient Roman god of medicine (known in Greek as Asclepius), whose staff, about which is curled a snake, is commonly used as a symbol of medicine.

60 *Elysian*: In Greek mythology the Elysian Fields, or Elysium, are the final resting place of heroes; the word is often used to mean 'heavenly'.

68 *Niobe in Distress… Mr Richard Wilson*: In Greek mythology, Niobe's children were murdered by the deities Artemis and Apollo. Niobe's tragedy is told in the works of the Roman poet, Ovid (*c*.43 BC–*c*. AD 18), and in *The Destruction of the Children of Niobe*, a 1760 painting by the Welsh landscape painter Richard Wilson (1714–1782).

68 *The Phrygian queen… Maeonia*: Niobe's father, Tantalus, was often referred to as King of Phrygia, although his kingdom was actually in Anatolia, which later became Lydia. Maeonia was the original name of the Lydian kingdom.

68 *Dodonean Jove*: Jove is another name for Jupiter, the Roman god of the sky and thunder; Dodona was an ancient Greek town and shrine. This is possibly a reference to Homer's *Odyssey*, Book XIX, in which Ulysses 'journey'd thence to Dodonean Jove; By the sure precept of the sylvan shrine'.

68 *Her grandsire Atlas… sky*: Niobe's mother's name is generally given as Dione, the daughter of Atlas, a Titan who was condemned for his part in the Titans' revolt against Zeus to hold up the heavens

NOTES

for the rest of eternity. Niobe's father, Tantalus, was the son of Zeus, making Zeus, king of the gods and god of thunder and the sky, her 'other grandsire'.

69 *Manto*: In Greek mythology, Manto was the daughter of the prophet Tireseus; she was a Theban oracle and later priestess to Hera, wife of Zeus and goddess of women.

69 *Latona*: Latona is the Roman equivalent of Leto, the mother of Apollo and Artemis.

70 *Venus*: The Roman goddess of love.

70 *Coeus' offspring*: Coeus, a Titan, was Leto's father.

70 *Cadmus*: The first King of Thebes.

70 *Delos*: A Greek island – the birthplace of Apollo and Artemis.

71 *Cynthus*: Mount Cynthus is a rock on the island of Delos, thought to be the centre of ancient civilisation on the island.

71 *Juno*: The Roman goddess of marriage.

71 *Ismenus*: The list of Niobe and Amphion's children is inconsistent between various sources, but most name six or seven of each sex; Ismenus, the first killed, is the eldest.

73 *the Delian god*: A god from Delos, i.e. Apollo.

75 *The queen of all... silent tears*: Although Wheatley's footnote declares the final verse to be 'the work of another hand', critics are not necessarily united in belief – no name was ever given, and John Wheatley insists that the poems are all the poet's own (see p. 122); some pose that the attribution of the verse to 'another hand' denies the story reaching Ovid's conclusion in the main body of the poem.

76 *Damon's tender sighs*: A reference to the Greek tale of Damon and Pythias, which was used to demonstrate the Pythagorean ideal of friendship – Damon offers himself as collateral so that Pythias, who has been charged with plotting against the ruler, can leave to settle his affairs, on the agreement that Damon will be executed in his stead if he does not return.

77 *the saint... Elisha's*: The references are to (as made clear in Wheatley's footnotes): Enoch, an ancestor of Noah, and Elijah and Elisha, who were prophets and miracle-workers of the ninth century BC.

- 79 *To Mrs S.W.*: This poem is addressed to Wheatley's mistress, Susanna Wheatley. (See also 'Ode to Neptune' on p. 52.)
- 80 *Hebe's mantle*: A reference to Hebe, the daughter of Hera and Zeus and goddess of eternal youth in Greek mythology. The mantle, or shawl, of Hebe is Wheatley's invention, but is clearly a metaphor for health.
- 82 *By I.B.*: This poem was printed in the original edition of the *Poems*, although, as the title indicates, it is not by Wheatley. It is believed to have been written by James Bowdoin II (1726–1790), an American Governor from Boston, Massachusetts. It was included in the collection so that Wheatley could answer the riddle (or 'rebus') it poses.
- 82 *Dardan*: An inhabitant of Troy – the ancient city located on the western edge of the Dardanelles strait.
- 83 *Helen*: A reference to the *Iliad*, in which Helen of Troy's affair with Paris, a prince of Troy, led to the Trojan War.
- 83 *Euphorbus… death resign*: In the *Iliad*, Menelaus, the Greek leader and Helen's husband, kills Euphorbus, a Trojan ally, for wounding Patroclus (see second note to p. 13).
- 83 *Quebec*: Wheatley solves the riddle in verse (the capitals are original, and give the answer): Quail, Unicorn, Emerald, Boston, Euphorbus, C——m (Chatham) – the initial capitals of which spell QUEBEC.

NOTES TO THE MEMOIR

- 85 *this little book*: i.e. the memoir, since this was first published on its own, in 1834.
- 87 *slavery came to an end in Massachusetts*: In Massachusetts – where the Wheatleys lived – in 1783, the *Commonwealth v. Nathaniel Jennison* case was brought to the Supreme Court, and the resulting ruling was that slaves had a constitutional right to liberty.
- 87 *Revolutionary War*: The American Revolutionary War, or War of Independence (1775–1783), resulted in the overthrow of British rule, and marked the establishment of the United States of America.
- 89 *filibeg*: A kilt.

NOTES

89 *How much... does not appear*: According to John Wheatley, in the letter which was published at the beginning of the *Poems* (see p. 122), Phillis learnt the English language 'to which she was an utter stranger before' in the months following her purchase by the Wheatleys.

90 *pouring out water... rising*: It is now thought that this is indicative of a Muslim background, as one of the pillars of Islam is praying five times a day, before which *wudu*, a purification ritual, is performed.

90 *One writer, who has treated of the life of Phillis*: A reference to Margaretta Odell, another biographer of Wheatley.

91 *belles-lettres*: Literally, 'fine letters' (French); used generally to mean 'literary studies'.

93 *guilty... their own*: 'Guilty of a skin/Not coloured like his own' is a line from *The Task* (1784) by William Cowper (1731–1800).

100 *embellished with an engraving... original*: The engraving is reproduced at the beginning of this volume.

102 *Mr Thacher... History of Plymouth*: A reference to *History of the Town of Plymouth: From Its First Settlement in 1620 to the Year 1832* (1835) by James Thacher (1754–1844).

103 *No stone... Revolution*: It is still unknown where Phillis was buried, although sources suggest that she was buried in an unmarked grave at either the Granary Burying Ground or Copp's Hill Burying Ground. However, in 2003, a memorial to Phillis was erected on the Commonwealth Avenue Mall in Boston.

NOTES TO THE APPENDIX

122 *Rev. Mr Occom, the Indian Minister*: A reference to the Reverend Samson Occom (1723–92), a Presbyterian cleric and the first Native American to be published in English.

123 *the following page*: i.e. the contents page of the original edition.

123 *DD*: *Divinitatis Doctor* ('Doctor of Divinity', Latin).

INDEX OF FIRST LINES

A bird delicious to the taste	82
Adieu, New England's smiling meads	79
All-Conquering Death! by thy resistless pow'r	77
Apollo's wrath to man the dreadful spring	68
Arise, my soul, on wings enraptur'd rise	33
Attend my lays, ye ever honour'd nine	41
Ere yet the morn its lovely blushes spread	18
From dark abodes to fair ethereal light	22
Grim monarch! see, depriv'd of vital breath	24
Hail, happy day, when, smiling like the morn	50
Hail, happy saint, on thine immortal throne	20
Indulgent muse! my grov'lling mind inspire	53
Lo! for this dark terrestrial ball	64
Maecenas, you, beneath the myrtle shade	13
Mneme begin. Inspire, ye sacred nine	44
No more the flow'ry scenes of pleasure rife	63
O'erwhelming sorrow now demands my song	56
On Death's domain intent I fix my eyes	57
O thou bright jewel, in my aim I strive	15
Say, heav'nly muse, what king or mighty god	43
Say, muse divine, can hostile scenes delight	50
Soon as the sun forsook the eastern main	42
The poet asks, and Phillis can't refuse	83
Though thou did'st hear the tempest from afar	55
Through airy roads he wings his instant flight	48
Through thickest glooms look back, immortal shade	59
Thy various works, imperial queen, we see	46

To cultivate in ev'ry noble mind	61
To show the lab'ring bosom's deep intent	75
'Twas mercy brought me from my pagan land	18
We trace the pow'r of Death from tomb to tomb	38
Where contemplation finds her sacred spring	39
While an intrinsic ardour prompts to write	16
While deep you mourn beneath the cypress shade	66
While others chant of gay Elysian scenes	60
While raging tempests shake the shore	52
Who taught thee conflict with the pow'rs of night	23
Ye martial pow'rs, and all ye tuneful nine	26
Your subjects hope, dread sire	17

APPENDIX

PREFACE

From the first edition of the poems

The following poems were written originally for the amusement of the author, as they were the products of her leisure moments. She had no intention ever to have published them – nor would they now have made their appearance, but at the importunity of many of her best and most generous friends, to whom she considers herself as under the greatest obligations.

As her attempts in poetry are now sent into the world, it is hoped the critic will not severely censure their defects; and we presume they have too much merit to be cast aside with contempt as worthless and trifling effusions.

As to the disadvantages she has laboured under with regard to learning, nothing needs to be offered, as her master's letter in the following page will sufficiently show the difficulties in this respect she had to encounter.

With all their imperfections, the *Poems* are now humbly submitted to the perusal of the public.

1773

The following is a copy of a letter sent by the author's master to the publisher.

Phillis was brought from Africa to America in the year 1761, between seven and eight years of age. Without any assistance from school education, and by only what she was taught in the family, she, in sixteen months' time from her arrival, attained the English language, to which she was an utter stranger before, to such a degree as to read any the most difficult parts of the Sacred Writings, to the great astonishment of all who heard her.

As to her writing, her own curiosity led her to it, and this she learnt in so short a time that, in the year 1765, she wrote a letter to the Rev. Mr Occom, the Indian Minister,* while in England.

She has a great inclination to learn the Latin tongue, and has made some progress in it. This relation is given by her master who bought her, and with whom she now lives.

— JOHN WHEATLEY, 1772

NOTICE TO THE PUBLIC

From the first edition of the poems

As it has been repeatedly suggested to the Publisher by persons who have seen the manuscript that numbers would be ready to suspect they were not really the writings of Phillis, he has procured the following attestation from the most respectable characters in Boston, that none might have the least ground for disputing their original.

We whose names are underwritten do assure the world that the poems specified in the following page* were (as we verily believe) written by Phillis, a young Negro girl, who was but a few years since brought an uncultivated Barbarian from Africa, and has ever since been, and now is, under the disadvantage of serving as a slave in a family in this town. She has been examined by some of the best judges, and is thought qualified to write them.

His Excellency Thomas Hutchinson, Governor
The Hon. Andrew Oliver, Lieutenant-Governor

The Hon. Thomas Hubbard   The Rev. Charles Chauncey, DD*
The Hon. John Erving   The Rev. Mather Byles, DD
The Hon. James Pitts   The Rev. Ed. Pemberton, DD
The Hon. Harrison Gray   The Rev. Andrew Elliot, DD

The Hon. James Bowdoin	The Rev. Samuel Cooper, DD
John Hancock, Esq.	The Rev. Mr Samuel Mather
Joseph Green, Esq.	The Rev. Mr John Moorhead
Richard Carey, Esq.	Mr John Wheatley, her Master

NB: The original attestation, signed by the above gentlemen, may be seen by applying to Archibald Bell, Bookseller, No. 8, Aldgate Street.

— ARCHIBALD BELL, 1773

NOTICE TO THE PUBLIC

From the first edition of the memoir

The Publisher, in presenting the following memoir to the public, ventures to call the attention of its readers to the motives with which it has been prepared, and to the design in the execution of which it has been intended as the first step.

The Publisher now entertains the project of a series of similar publications, and embraces, with great pleasure, this occasion of announcing to that large and increasing portion of the community who are benevolently interested in the condition and prospects of our coloured brethren that he has been able already to effect such arrangements as will enable him, as he confidently trusts, to render these publications equally instructive and interesting to all of this class of readers, and especially to the young, without giving just cause of dissatisfaction or displeasure to any. It is intended, as far as possible, to avoid every subject of a controversial nature, and to concentrate the efforts of those concerned wholly upon the grand object of presenting anecdotes and traits of the history, biography, capacity and condition of the race of which we speak to the consideration of the friends of that race, and to the study of the youthful intellect, in such a manner as to promote as far as may be clear, unprejudiced and enlightened views of the whole subject.

Of the various subjects which will be treated of in this series it is unnecessary to speak more particularly, as these will be left for the most part to the judgement and taste of the respective writers, with no other restriction than may seem to be implied by the principles above stated. In addition to the individual who has furnished the first of the course, the Publisher is happy to announce that he has secured the services of several distinguished authors, both male and female, and he trusts that their established character will be deemed to furnish a sufficient guarantee of the faithful and able performance of so much of his plan, at least, as shall depend upon their contributions.

The Publisher would suppose it a work of supererogation to point out the benefits which may be reasonably expected to arise from these publications in their effect on the young. It must be, under circumstances now existing in the country, that a curiosity will be felt by this class in the subjects which these essays will discuss. How desirable is it that such curiosity should be gratified by aliment which shall be not only unexceptionable in regard to its influence on both the heart and the head, but shall possess also the merit of conveying information of a valuable kind, selected, simplified and prepared with especial reference to the taste and necessities of this numerous and important class of readers. Such an end, it is confidently hoped, will be attained by the series of which this memoir is the commencement.

— GEORGE W. LIGHT, 1834

www.ingramcontent.com/pod-product-compliance
Lightning Source LLC
Chambersburg PA
CBHW030911080526
44589CB00010B/249